CARD MANIPULATIONS
SERIES 1-5

Jean Hugard

CARD MANIPULATIONS
SERIES 1-5

DOVER PUBLICATIONS, INC.
New York

Published in Canada by General Publishing Company, Ltd., 30 Lesmill Road, Don Mills, Toronto, Ontario.

This Dover edition, first published in 1973, is an unabridged, slightly altered republication of the series originally published by Max Holden, New York City, between 1934 and 1936. The publisher gratefully acknowledges the cooperation of the University of Texas Library which lent a copy of this work for reproduction.

International Standard Book Number: 0-486-20539-8
Library of Congress Catalog Card Number: 73-81508

Manufactured in the United States of America
Dover Publications, Inc.
180 Varick Street
New York, N. Y. 10014

CONTENTS

(Each series contains its own detailed table of contents.)

SERIES 1 AND 2

Card Manipulation No. 1 and 2

By JEAN HUGARD

ONE HAND TOP CARD PALM

A description of a method of palming the top card of the pack appeared in the Magic Wand some years ago. The following is that adopted by the writer. Once mastered, it will be found to be the best way to palm off a single card from the top. The sleight can be done with either hand with equal facility. It is best to learn it with the right hand first.

Hold the pack, well squared, face down in your right hand, the first joint of the thumb at the inner end and the top joints of your first three fingers at the outer end, the tip of the little finger resting on the outer right hand corner. (Fig. 1).

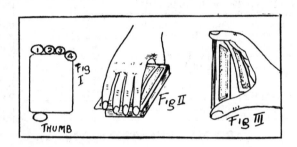

Press the tip of your little finger on the corner of the top card and push it slightly off the pack. (Fig. 2.) In the figure the projection of the top corner is exaggerated for the sake of clearness. Now press the finger tip down on the projecting corner of the card and it will spring up into the palm.

A little difficulty may be found at first in freeing the rear edges of the card from the thumb, hence the necessity for bending the tip of the thumb slightly inward. In practice the four fingers are pressed close together at the end of the pack, the little finger tip is moved to the corner of the top card, pushing it out very slightly, then it is immediately replaced at the end of the pack, which action levers the card up into the palm.

The sleight can be done in the act of handing the pack out to be shuffled and is imperceptible.

THE HINDU SHUFFLE OR RUNNING CUT

I have dubbed this very useful series of moves "The Hindu Shuffle" because it was first shown to me over thirty years ago by a Hindu magacian. Since then I have never seen a Hindu performer use any other kind of shuffle. Passing strange if the despised Indian juggler has given his vastly superior Western confreres another valuable legacy.

You hold the pack face down on the left hand, the top left corner near the base of the thumb, first finger tip at the middle of its outer end and the other three fingers at the outer side of the deck.

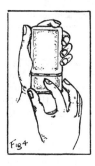

Grasping the inner end of the pack with the tips of the right thumb and second finger you pull out all the cards except a small packet on the top. This is held back by the tip of your left second finger pressing these cards against the base of the thumb (Fig. 4). In this action both hands move, the left hand a few inches outward, the right hand a few inches in the opposite direction. The packet thus drawn off you let fall on your left palm by releasing the grip of your left thumb and second finger.

You bring your right hand, with the rest of the pack, back over this packet to the same position that it originally had, and then you repeat the action by drawing off a second small packet from the top in exactly the same way.

This packet is allowed to fall on top of the first and the tip of the left forefinger acts as a stop, keeping the outer ends of the deck squared.

Successive packets are thus pulled off into the left hand until the cards in the right hand are exhausted.

THE HINDU SHUFFLE AS A SUBSTITUTE FOR THE PASS

This shuffle may be used by the magician as a powerful weapon to use in controlling a card, or cards, which have been returned to the deck by members of the audience, which he apparently loses among the rest of the cards by a thorough shuffle.

To do this by means of the two-handed pass the textbooks instruct the student to divide the pack into two portions, have the chosen card replaced on the lower part, then make the pass, false shuffle retaining the card on top. Again make the pass, bringing it to the middle, cut at that point, have the second selected card placed on the first, again make the pass, false shuffle, and so on and on, for as many cards as have been drawn. To make the pass cleanly is a difficult operation and to control four cards by the method outlined, you would have to do it seven times and false shuffle four times.

The use of the Hindu shuffle to attain the same end is so much easier and cleaner that I have no doubt that having tried it once you will "use no other".

Let us suppose that a card has been chosen and you are about to have it replaced in the pack. Holding the pack in position for the Hindu shuffle you pull off two or three packets into your left hand, as described, advancing toward the person who drew the card. "Kindly replace your card in the pack," you say, "anywhere you like," and you pull off another small packet, then extend your left hand towards him.

He will naturally put his card on top of those in your left hand, you immediately bring the cards in your right hand on top of it and continue the process of pulling small packets off the top of the pack, letting them fall on those in the left hand.

Nothing could appear to be fairer and, to the audience, the card is lost among the others; in reality, you have it on the top of the pack. This is how you do it: When you bring the right hand packet on top of the chosen card, just replaced, you pick up the rear end of that card with the tips of the right third finger and thumb, holding it concealed under the other cards in the right hand.

It is immaterial whether you pick up one, two or three cards from the packet on your left hand, therefore there is no hesitation or change in the tempo of the action. You hold a small division, or break, between this picked up card, or cards, and the rest of the cards, at the back. This break is not visible from the front, but it enables you to draw off all the cards above it cleanly by the sense of touch alone, leaving the picked up card, or cards, only, between the thumb and second finger, to be dropped on the top of the pack as the last move in the shuffle.

The actual pick up is completely covered by the action of pulling off another packet from the top of the pack and letting it fall on the left hand, apparently on top of the selected card. You continue pulling off small packets until you are warned by the break that only the picked up chosen card remains and you drop this on the others. You have the selected card on top.

To collect and control several cards by this method, you proceed as described above to get the first card to the top. Then, as you go to the second person, you pull out about two-thirds of the pack, allowing the top third to fall on your left hand. The second card is replaced on this, i. e. on top of the first card. You continue the action exactly as before, except, of course, that you must pick up at least two cards.

You will readily see that no matter how many cards have been selected the action is simply a repetition of what is to all appearances an honest shuffle, yet at the conclusion you have all the cards on the top of the pack. You must remember, however, that they are in the reverse order to that in which they were chosen.

～⦿～

AND YET AGAIN — THE RISING CARDS

No apology is needed for this attack on the Rising Cards. It remains the best effect possible with cards. The new twists here described add to the mystery.

A small fake is required. This is a long thin black hat pin, on the blunt end of which is soldered a little cup in which you put a dab of magician's wax. The pin you push into your right sleeve on the side nearest your body, so that the cup is near your wrist on the outside of your sleeve. Under the lower edge of your vest near the middle you have a thick piece of cork.

THE EFFECT:—Freely selected cards rise from the pack and the last, not only rises, but remains suspended without support.

THE METHOD:—You have the pack shuffled and allow three cards to be chosen freely. These are returned to the pack and you bring them to the top by means, let us say, of the Hindu Shuffle. It will strengthen the effect if you palm off the three cards and have the pack shuffled by a spectator, but this is not absolutely necessary.

The top card, which will be that drawn by the third person and returned to the pack last, you cause to rise by the old method, you hold the pack in your right hand, squarely facing the audience, and you push the card up with the tip of your forefinger.

You make a false shuffle and take the pack in your left hand, upright, the bottom card facing the front; the back of your left hand covers the lower half of the deck. You secretly push about half the rear cards of the pack about one quarter of an inch downward, making a step, visible from the back, but not to the audience. (Fig. 5-A).

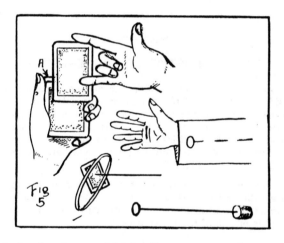

You rub the tip of your right forefinger on your sleeve, then lay it on top of the pack and slowly lift it. Nothing happens. You repeat the rubbing more vigorously and again apply your forefinger tip to the cards. This time the second chosen card rises from the pack apparently attached to the finger tip.

You do this by straightening the little finger of your right hand behind the pack and with its tip you push up the rear card. You raise the card slowly and, as soon as its lower end clears the top of the step between the two packets (the pack is divided) you push it forward against the top of the front packet, then, with your little finger you push the rear packet up flush with the other.

You now have the card clipped between the two packets and you can turn the pack sideways to show that the card has really risen from the middle. You go over to drawer of the card and request him to remove it himself. In returning to your position before the audience you seize the cup of the fake and draw it out behind the pack with ease, then clip it with the fingers of your left hand. With your right hand you adjust the front of your vest and, under cover of doing that, you guide the point of the pin to the cork. You push the pin home by drawing your left hand back toward the body and so attach the rear card to the wax. This card you now cause to rise, apparently in the same way as the last, by the attraction of your fingertip, but in reality you gently lower the pack, the card remains stationary, but the illusion is perfect.

You now remove your left hand with the pack and the card remains suspended from your finger tip. The climax is reached when you remove your finger from the card and it remains in the air like Mahomet's coffin.

To get rid of the fake, you replace the pack in front of the floating card, with your left thumb detach it from the waxed end of the fake. Bring your right hand over to the pack, take the card and toss it to a spectator. In doing this you bring your right forearm in front of the left hand and the cards. With the left fingers behind the pack pull out the pin and thrust it into your right coat sleeve in its original position.

While the card is suspended a hoop can be passed over it if so desired.

AN EASY SUBSTITUTE FOR THE PASS

This is a simplification of the Charlier one hand·pass. You hold the pack by its sides at the tip of the thumb on one side and the tips of the second and third fingers on the other. As you advance the pack toward a spectator, inviting him to replace a card he has previously drawn, you allow the lower half of the pack to fall into the fork of your left thumb. (Fig. 6-A). You have the card placed in the opening thus made and at once drop the upper packet on top of it. (Fig. 6-B).

This procedure looks perfectly fair, but in dropping the top packet you pushed it out a little so that instead of falling squarely on the lower packet, it lies a little to one side, so making a step between the two packets (Fig. 6-B). The chosen card is on top of the lower packet.

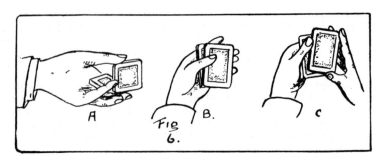

A   Fig 6.   B.   C

You proceed at once to an overhand shuffle. As you take the pack in your right hand your left thumb falls naturally on the back of the chosen card, and you pull it out in the first movement of the shuffle. (Fig. 6-C). You then shuffle off the rest of the cards on top of it in the regular way. The chosen card is thus brought to the bottom of the deck and can be disposed of as may be necessary for the trick in hand.

RELATIVITY AND CARDS

Among the best of comparatively recent card tricks is one wherein two initialled cards change places under apparently impossible conditions, for no duplicates are used. The only drawback to this mystery is the fact that a special card is necessary, which takes it out of the most favored class of card tricks, those that can be done with a borrowed deck at any time. To remedy this the following method has been devised.

THE EFFECT:—Two cards freely chosen are marked, one with a spectator's initials, the other with those of the performer. Each card is placed in a pocket of the person whose initials it bears, yet they change places and are removed by the spectators themselves. Here is one place where that much overworked expression, "a knock-out," might be used in truth.

THE METHOD:—Any pack of cards may be employed and the only preparation necessary is for you to take any one card, preferably not a court card or a card with many spots on it, say a four or a six of any suit, and write your initials plainly in pencil on its face.

Having done this put the initialled card face up on top of the deck. Take any other card and place it, also face up, on top of this initialled card and, finally, take any other card and put it face down on these two.

This is the way things stand just prior to beginning the trick. On top of the pack you have a card face down, under it a card face up, and under this again, that is third from the top, is a card bearing your initials, also face up.

You begin by false shuffling the pack. This can be done by either the riffle or the overhand method. If you use a riffle you must be careful not to allow anyone to get a glimpse of the reversed cards. Spread the pack and allow a spectator to choose a card. Do not say, "You notice I do not force a card on you," or anything of the kind. Be satisfied to allow it to be seen that a free choice is given. It is fair enough to give the person the option of replacing his card and taking another if he desires it. That is convincing enough without suggesting to your audience that there is such a thing as forcing a card.

As soon as a card has been taken you separate the inner ends of the three top cards with the ball of your thumbs and slip the tip of your left little finger under them.

You take the card from the drawer and let everyone see what card it is, then place it face up on top of the deck. You ask him what his initials are and write them plainly on the face of his card in pencil. Let us suppose he has chosen the eight of diamonds.

You turn the card face down, lift it off the pack with your right hand and place it in the person's inside coat pocket. Or, rather, that is what you appear to do. In reality, thanks to the break held by your left little finger, you have turned the four top cards, as one, thus bringing the card with your initials on it, the four of spades, to the top, and this is the card you put in the spectator's pocket.

Naturally you must not allow anyone to see the face of this card. To avoid doing so when putting the card in the spectator's pocket, you keep it face down until you have it inside his coat, then turn the card so that its face is toward the cloth and only its back is visible as you drop it into the pocket.

You have succeeded in getting your initialled card into the spectator's pocket, it remains for you to place his initialled card in your own pocket with all apparent fairness. The method by which you manage this is ingenious.

The other initialled card is now face down, third from the top, just above it is an indifferent card face up and on top of the pack is a card face down. This is the natural result of your having turned four cards, as one, to bring your card on top. You must now bring these three cards to the middle of the pack. So you undercut about half the deck and shuffle the lower portion on top in a perfectly fair and open manner.

Explaining that one more card has to be selected and that you wish to have it done so that all can see that the selection is purely haphazard, you say that you will have someone put the pack behind his back, which you do to illustrate what is to be done. He is then to take off the top card and put it on the bottom of the pack, take the next one and reversing it, push it into the deck somewhere about the middle.

The moment you placed the pack behind you, you took off the top card, turned over the next one, replaced the top card face down, and brought the pack forward again. You merely gave an illustration of what is to be done, or so it seems to the audience.

You have someone stand alongside you and again instruct him what he is to do. Then put the pack face down in his left hand and gently guide his hand behind his back.

"Remember," you say, "Put the top card on the bottom. Someone might suspect me of knowing what that card is. Turn the next card face up and push it right into the pack. Done? Thank you." You take the pack.

"Somewhere in this pack is a card under the one that this gentleman has placed face up. That is the card we will use to complete the experiment. I can think of no fairer way of selecting a card. No one, not even this gentleman himself, can have the faintest idea of what card it is."

You spread the pack, exposing the reversed card, and you take out the card below it. It is, of course, the first card that was chosen, the eight of diamonds, on which you placed the person's initials. (The card the spectator reversed he merely righted in so doing.) You look at it, holding it face towards you. "The four of spades," you say. You hand the pack to the spectator beside you asking him to run through it and satisfy himself that the four of spades and the eight of diamonds have been taken out. This will keep him busy while you pretend to write your initials on the card, which you then place in your pocket.

The trick is done, you have only to bring out the effect. Addressing the person who has the pack, you say, "You do not find either of those cards? How could you when this gentleman has the eight of diamonds in his pocket and I have the four of spades in mine? I merely wished to have no loophole left for any suspicion of unfair play. What is about to take place is an example of Relativity. They say that only half a dozen people besides Einstein himself understand his theory. Well, I won't attempt to explain it, I'll just prove it. The celebrated Erasmus of Rotterdam, maintained that a thing can only be in one place at one time. That was true in his time, but after all truth is only relative. These two cards will disintegrate and reintegrate, I mean they will go to pieces, and then pull themselves together again in such a minute fraction of time that practically, they are in two places at one time. Are you ready, sir? Go. Will you take the card from your pocket? You have the four of spades? It has my initials on it? Will you take this other card from my pocket yourself? It is your eight of diamonds with your initials on it. Now you must be satisfied that Relativity is a Fact."

Properly performed or presented, this trick is as near to a real magical effect as can be conceived. A fastidious performer may object to one point, that of putting the pack behind your back to reverse the second card. The expert will have his own way of avoiding this perhaps inartistic feature. The following is an easy and practical alternative.

After you have shuffled the reversed card and the first chosen card to the middle, you stand with your right side to the audience and you square the pack by running your right thumb and fingers along its ends. You palm the top card and move your hand to the outer edge of the pack. With the left thumb push the next card a little off the pack to the right, just far enough to catch its edge against the right forefinger. In the act of bringing the right hand back over the pack you turn the card over and leave the palmed card on top of it. The turn is covered by the back of the right hand and a trial before a mirror will show how simple the move is. After reversing the card you repeat the squaring movement very openly, running the ends of the pack through the right fingers and thumb, then the sides between the fingers and thumb of the left hand.

(Credit for the effect must go to the talented inventor, Annemann. The only kudos now claimed is for its adaptation to a borrowed deck, that is by the elimination of the prepared card.)

THE BURGLARS. A STORY TRICK

In this story trick the four Jacks figure as burglars. It is advisable, though not absolutely necessary to have them in order of Spades, Hearts, Diamonds, Clubs, from the top, and to have a few cards between each one. This may be done in a moment or two by spreading the pack fanwise, finding the Jacks by their indices, and altering their positions as may be necessary.

Suppose this is done. You take the pack face up in your left hand, saying that you require the four Jacks. You run through the cards, pushing them off one by one into the right hand, till you come to the Jack of Clubs. Lift off the cards in your right hand and turn those in your left toward the spectators, showing the Jack. Push it slightly off the pack and bring the cards in your right hand over it again, but raise them so that this time they cover only the upper half of the Jack. (Fig. 7-A). Grip it at the back with the tip of the right second finger and then bring the right hand packet down flush with the rest of the pack. The result will be that the Jack of Clubs will protrude half its length below the deck. (Fig. 7-B).

This should be done fairly and openly. You have simply found the first Jack and you have pushed it halfway out of the pack.

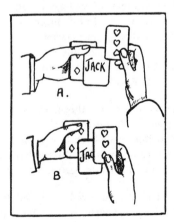

You continue to run over the faces of the cards until you come to the Jack of Diamonds. Here the trickery begins. Before you lift off the right hand packet to show the Diamond Jack you push the next card squarely behind it, then push the two as one, a little off the pack as you did the Club Jack. Remove the right hand packet and show the Jack of Diamonds. You hold it squarely towards spectators and they have no reason to suspect anything if you work easily and smoothly.

Bring the right hand packet on the upper half of this Jack (and the indifferent card concealed behind it) and clip the two cards, as one, with the tip of your right second finger as you did the first Jack. Again bring the right hand packet down flush with the rest of the cards. You now have two Jacks protruding below the pack, and the second one has an indifferent card concealed behind it.

The third Jack, the Jack of Hearts, you treat in exactly the same way as the second, that is to say, you secure the card following it and bring them both down together as one card.

The last card, the Jack of Spades, you push out alone, and here to make your previous actions more convincing, you may "accidentally" let it fall on the table. In picking it up you cause it to protrude with the other three. Run through the remaining cards quickly, close up the pack in your left hand, holding it facing the audience, and daintily pull out the protruding Jacks. If you hold the ends of the cards firmly this is perfectly safe, and, since you have not squared the pack exactly, parts of the faces of all four Jacks will show.

Properly done, no one can have any suspicion that you have anything more than the four Jacks. However, you do not hesitate. You at once hand the pack to a spectator asking him to take out the King of Clubs. "These four Jacks", you say, "are four bold bad burglars, and, if you can exercise sufficient imagination, please try to think of the pack as the residence of one of our multi-millionaires, one of those who hasn't paid any income tax. The burglars have planned a raid." You square the Jacks and lay the packet on top of the pack which you hold face down in your left hand.

"The first one, the Jack of Spades, goes into the basement, ready for any dirty work he may have to do." You turn the top card over, show it is the Jack of Spades, take it off and put it on the bottom of the pack. Lift the pack squarely to the audience to show it. To do this you grip the pack between right thumb at the inner end, second and third fingers at the outer end. This by way of illustration that the cards should always be held as openly and as much in full view as possible, and graceful gestures should be cultivated.

In addition to being graceful, however, you have taken the opportunity to lift the inner ends of the two top cards a little with the ball of the right thumb. You do this by sense of touch alone, there is no need to look at the cards.

Replace the pack face down in your left hand and at once slip the tip of your left little finger between the two top cards and the rest of the deck. These two cards, you will remember, are an indifferent card followed by the Jack of Hearts. You turn these two as one card, showing the Jack of Hearts.

"This Jack", you continue, "has been assigned to the living rooms on account of his taking ways. In case of accident his appearance will carry him through as he is used to mixing with the elite." You turn the two cards down, take off the top card, the indifferent card, and push it in the lower third part of the deck.

The Jack of Hearts is now on the top and you have to get that card out of the way. You take the pack in your right hand, turn it over and show the Jack of Spades. "Still doing spade work in the basement," you remark. Turn the cards down again on the left hand, pushing off the top card, the Jack of Hearts, with the left thumb into the right palm, and immediately afterward drawing it under the pack by extending the left fingers. The action is covered by turning the back of the right hand to the audience, and then squaring the pack with the usual motion of the hand.

"We have two of the rascals in action," you continue, and as you talk you again separate the inner ends of the two top cards ready for the pick-up as one card. "Here is the third, the Jack of Diamonds. Being a specialist in precious stones he is sent to ransack the bedrooms." You turn over the two cards as one, showing the Jack of Diamonds, turn them down again, and, taking off the indifferent card, you insert it in the upper third of the pack. You are, of course, careful not to allow anyone to see the faces of the cards actually placed in the pack.

You now have two Jacks on the top, the Jack of Diamonds and under it the Jack of Clubs. Once more you turn two as one showing the Jack of Clubs. "This fellow, being an athlete, all ready for a rough and tumble, enters the house through the roof." You take the top card, face to yourself, then lift the edge of the next card so that its back is to the spectators, and put the card under it. "He finds a convenient trap door and in he goes."

"Unfortunately for the gang, an alarm is raised. A phone call goes through to the Police Station and — may I trouble you for that King of Clubs? — Here is the Sergeant. He rushes up the fire escape to take the rascals in the rear. (Put the King on top of the pack). There is a general commotion" — You cut the pack — "and with his usual success, we find he has captured the whole gang." Run through the cards, faces to the front and show the King with two Jacks on each side of him.

ANOTHER VERSION

The following more elaborate version requires the use of duplicate Jacks and King of Clubs, but the enhanced effect makes the extra trouble worth while.

In addition to the duplicates two rubber bands are necessary. These are the thin kind and should be well stretched beforehand. Their tension should be so weakened that either can be stretched around the length and breadth of a card without bending it. A knot must be tied in the middle of each band so that each has two loops. These are to represent handcuffs in the story.

To prepare, you place the four duplicate Jacks on the back of the extra King of Clubs, then stretch one of the rubber bands around the five cards, one loop lengthways, the other sideways, the knot coming in the middle of the face of the King. This packet you put in your top outside coat pocket, face of the King outward. It should be just out of sight but within reach of your fingertips. If your pocket is a deep one the packet may be brought to the correct height by placing a small silk hand-herchief at the bottom of the pocket. The second rubber band you have with the deck.

You begin by stripping out the Jacks as has been described already and have the King of Clubs removed by a spectator. Place the Jacks in your left hand and take back the King. Stretch the rubber loops over it in exactly the same way as you did over the duplicate King, bringing the knot in the middle of its face.

You tell your audience that the King is a local Police Captain and that your pocket is to be regarded as the police station. You push the card into your pocket behind the packet already there, but the moment it is out of sight you seize the end of the duplicate King of Clubs and bring it into view. You fix your handkerchief in such a way that about half an inch of the packet will protrude from the pocket.

The manipulation of the Jacks is exactly the same as before, up to the point where you have two at the top and two at the bottom. You have now to get rid of these four Jacks by palming them off the pack. There are many ways of doing this. Here is one:

At this point the patter runs that the marauders were discovered and a commotion ensued. To illustrate this you shuffle the cards thus—run two cards from the top to the bottom thus bringing all four to the bottom, then shuffle the whole pack but throw the last packet on the bottom. With your left hand palm off the four bottom cards and retain the pack in that hand for the moment. Thrust your right hand, letting it be seen that it is empty, into your right trouser pocket.. Bring the hand out and take the pack from your left hand. With the remark, "Where did I put that King of Clubs?", thrust your left hand into your left trouser pocket and leave the palmed cards there.

Then look down at your coat pocket, take the pack again in your left hand and remove the King of Clubs with your right hand. "Ah, here he is. Let's see what he can do." You hold the packet and the pack squarely facing the spectators and slowly push the packet into the middle of the pack. You hand the cards face up to a person to hold, saying you are confident that in four seconds, the Chief will have captured the whole band.

Tell him to run over the faces of the cards and look for the Jacks. When he comes to the King of Clubs quickly remove it and hold it at the tips of your fingers, face to the front. "Well, here is our noble captain anyway. He still has his handcuffs and that's something these days." The spectator fails to find any of the Jacks in the pack.

"Isn't that the usual thing. A clean get-away and the police searching for clues as always. Hello, what's this? Why he's got 'em after all and securely handcuffed to himself." You turn the King of Clubs sideways and show the cards on the back by riffling a corner. Then have a spectator remove the "handcuffs" and show the four Jacks to everyone.

If the spectator notices the extra thickness of the King, let him discover the Jacks himself, but be sure to make him hold the packet up so that all can see how they are secured.

THE MODERN DOVETAIL SHUFFLE

In the old original version of the dovetail shuffle, several selected cards were pushed into the pack diagonally, then straightened at the back of the pack so that their ends protruded an inch or so. The student was instructed to seize these protruding ends, pull the cards out of the deck, and then place them on the top or bottom as might be required for the trick. A difficult operation to do imperceptibly, unless the spectators obligingly looked the other way.

The modern version is not only easier, but, during its performance there is nothing to cover up, a rare delight in sleights. The cards are simply pushed into the pack, well separated, and you proceed to shuffle, the cards are all together and under control immediately.

Let us suppose that you are using four cards, which have been removed from the pack. You can fan the deck in your left hand with the faces outward, and press firmly on the back of the fan with your left thumb. Take up the four cards, one by one, and insert them in the pack at the top edge of the fan, allowing at least three quarters of each card to protrude. The firm grip maintained by your left thumb will hold the cards securely in position. (Fig. 9).

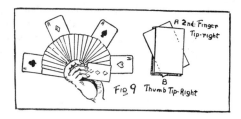

You show the cards thus, then close the fan with your right hand on to your left, gripping the pack at the middle of its sides between the tip of the thumb on one side and the tips of the second and third fingers on the other. The four protruding cards now lie one on the other. You bring your right hand, the fingers spread and extended so that the side of your third finger strikes against their outer sides. The tip of the second finger falls on the top of the four cards and your third finger is on the far side of them.

With these three fingers push the four cards a little to the left, then by pressing downward with the second finger tip push them diagonally through the pack until you feel the inner left corners strike the ball of your right thumb at the bottom of the pack. Now move the tip of your right second finger on to the opposite corners which protrude a little from the top of the deck. (Fig. 9).

Without removing the right hand you turn the pack upward to the position for the overhand shuffle; the ball of your right thumb still presses on the lower projecting corners of the four cards, and the tip of the right second finger secures the diagonally opposite corners of the same cards which protrude at the top of the pack. The four cards are thus held firmly between the right thumb and second finger and you could lift them out by one motion, but this must be done under cover of an overhand shuffle.

In lifting the pack with your right hand for the first movement in the shuffle you must press it between the right third finger on the face of the deck and the first finger on the back, otherwise all the cards but the gripped four will fall into the left hand at once. By relaxing the pressure of the first and third fingers you allow packets of cards to fall into your left hand as they are pulled off by the left thumb, exactly as in the regular shuffle. The four diagonally placed cards will be found to cling to the fingers to the last, and the final movement of the shuffle is to drop them all together on the top of the pack.

Every action in this highly effective sleight is either a natural one or is completely under cover. Some little practice is necessary to hold the pack securely and shuffle freely, but that small trouble will be repaid a hundredfold by the mastery of one of the most useful sleights in the whole range of card magic. The fanning of the pack and the insertion of the four cards lend themselves to graceful motions, the effect is convincing to the audience, and the action is quick and snappy. What more could be required?

JUST ONCE MORE—THE ACES

The dovetail shuffle, just detailed, lends itself to an effective version of the four ace trick for close work, where quick, snappy action is necessary to impress your auditors.

You take out the aces, letting it be seen that there are no others in the pack, and you insert them in the fanned deck, in the manner described. The action continues in the same way, but as you throw the four aces on the top of the pack in the last movement of the shuffle, you slip the tip of your left little finger under them. You thus have a break between the four aces and the other cards, so that you are able to palm them off quickly without having to count them.

You hand the pack to a spectator to shuffle and at once thrust both hands into your trouser pockets. You fumble about in your left pocket with your left hand and look down at it, but bring the hand out empty. "That's funny," you say, "I thought I felt something." In the meantime your right hand in your right pocket has pushed off the undermost of the palmed aces from the others which you retain in the palm. Withdraw your right hand and at once thrust it into your vest at the top, again leave one ace and bring out the hand apparently empty, really with two aces still palmed. Reaching into your top left vest pocket you produce one ace, pulling it out at the fingertips and retaining the last one in the palm. "I thought something hit me. Here's another." You place your hand under your coat at the shoulder and bring out the ace. You are now able to let it be seen that your hand is empty before bringing the third ace from the right trouser pocket, and the last one you produce by thrusting your hand under the bottom of your vest and reaching up for it. In the meantime the person to whom you gave the pack to shuffle, finds that the aces really have left his hands.

Snappily done the trick is most effective. It seems impossible to the layman that four well separated cards could be located in short order, and their reproduction from different places forms a fitting climax, to be rewarded with a generous round of applause.

THOUGHT ANTICIPATED

This is a striking effect in which a principle is used that has been much neglected in recent years, the use of the faced pack.

This is what apparently happens. A spectator shuffles the deck and satisfies himself that it is well mixed and regular in every way. You then pass the cards one by one before his eye, from hand to hand, counting them as you do so, asking him to note any card and remember both it and the number at which it occurs. A second person then names any other number and you cause the card to transfer itself to that new position in the pack.

Do not confuse this feat with the ancient one wherein you begin the second count with the first number. Your second count is made from one and then on in regular order.

Here is the new method. You take the shuffled pack and pass the cards before the person's eyes, one by one, asking him to mentally select any card and to remember its number as you count them aloud. You do this slowly and deliberately so that a choice will be made before you reach, say fifteen. At that number you stop and replace the fifteen cards on the pack in the same order.

Turning to another spectator you ask him to think of any number, say between fifteen and thirty, this merely so that the effect may not be dragged out too long. Requesting both persons to think intently of their numbers you put the pack behind your back. You gaze earnestly at the two persons in turn as if you were engaged in some deep calculation.

All you really do is to divide the pack in halves and place them face to face. Turn the pack so that the original top cards become the lower half and bring the pack forward. You hold the cards ready to deal and you ask everyone to remember that the card and the numbers have been merely thought of, that you have asked no questions, so that, unless you have read their minds correctly, there is no way by which you could know the card or the numbers.

"What was your number?" you ask the first person. "Seven? I knew it," you say confidently. "Let me show you that it has left that position." You deal out six cards face down and turn over the seventh. It is of course, an indifferent card. "That is not your card, is it?" He agrees.

"Now," you turn to the second person. "What number did you think of? Twenty? I was sure of it. Let us see if the card has arrived there."

As soon as the second number is given you mentally subtract the first number from it and the result gives you the number of cards you must deal before you turn the pack over. In this case seven from twenty leaves thirteen, so you have to deal thirteen cards before you turn the pack and continue the count from the other side. You have already dealt seven cards, six remain to be dealt before you reverse the deck. You continue dealing and when you reach the thirteenth card, pause before placing that card down. Holding it in your right hand you say:

"Thirteen is my unlucky number. Does this happen to be your card?" You throw it face up on the table. and at the same time drop your left hand a little, turning it so that the back of the hand is uppermost, thus turning the pack over.

"Not your card? Then I am sure I have succeeded. Don't name it yet." You continue the count deliberately, the cards now coming from the original top of the deck. On reaching the number twenty you place that card face down on the table apart from the others. You emphasize the fact that the card was selected mentally and the utter impossibility of the whole thing. The card is named and you slowly turn it over.

This trick has a bewildering effect on an audience. The necessary turn of the pack is made when the spectators have no cause for any suspicion, and the last cards are dealt so fairly and openly that they can only give you all the credit for having worked a small miracle. You have merely to substract the first number from the second to arrive at the number at which the pack has to be turned and this number is always at your "unlucky number."

It only remains to right the pack so that it will be ready for the next trick. The neatest way to do this is to take advantage of the surprise caused by the appearance of the card thought of, to riffle the inner end of the deck until you come to the point at which the two packets come face to face. Slip the tip of your left little finger between them. Then grip the top half between the thumb and fingers of your right hand and let the left hand with the lower half drop an inch or so. Put the point of your left thumb under this lower packet and press it upward, causing the packet to turn over. At once bring the two packets together and again riffle the cards.

In the unlikely chance that someone has kept his eyes fixed on your hands the slight motion made will be under cover of the back of your right hand and will pass as part of the action of riffling.

An alternative method which is bold but out of which you can get some fun, is to riffle shuffle the two packets as they are, face to face, thus throwing the face up cards amongst those face down, but keeping a face down card on top. You hand the pack in this condition to a person to shuffle prior to doing another trick. Then you ask him what sort of a card handler he is and show him the mess he has got them into.

A NEW FORCE

This is an adaptation of the double lift move. You have the card you wish to force on the top of the pack.

False shuffle several times using the overhand method first, running the card to the bottom then back to the top, then the riffle shuffle. Having only one card to control you can make these shuffles convincing. In your last riffle you hold back the top card of the left hand portion so that it drops last, on top of the force card. You thus have this card second from the top.

Addressing a spectator you ask him to name any number, not too high in order not to waste time. As you speak, looking directly at the person, you lift the rear ends of the two top cards slightly with the ball of your right thumb and slip the tip of your left little finger under them. The pack is in your left hand, your right over it ready to deal.

Suppose eight is called for. "Eight," you say. "Very well, I will deal off eight cards." You push off the two separated cards, as one, taking them between the tips of the right thumb and first and second fingers of your right hand, counting "One". Push off the following cards, one at a time, receiving them under your thumb tip on top of the two already taken, counting "two, three, four, five, six, seven." At "seven" you stop. "Wait a moment. I am forgetting. I don't wish to see the card you have chosen, or even to touch it." You replace the seven cards (really there are eight, of which the force card is now the eighth) on the top of the pack and hand it to the spectator, asking him to count off seven cards, look at the eighth and note what it is.

You then proceed as may be necessary for the trick in hand. If you have to control the card, as he takes it out, you have him return the rest of the cards to you; if you do not have to keep the card in view you let him retain the pack and shuffle the card in as he pleases.

A word of caution is necessary. You must take care that no one gets a glimpse of the bottom card of the packet in your right hand. This is best avoided by standing with your right side to the front, thus keeping the backs of the cards to the spectators all the time the count is made.

THE BOOMERANG CARD

That pretty and effective ornamental sleight whereby a card tossed into the air returns to the performer and is caught at his finger tips, is rarely seen nowadays. Probably this is owing to the fact that to make the card return any considerable distance requires practice, and partly by the spread of the easy back hand move.

By combining the throwing sleight with the back hand move and part of the top change a striking effect may be obtained. That may sound a formidable combination but there is nothing to be afraid of.

First it is necessary to be able to throw a card a few feet into the air and make return to your hand. To do this you take a card between the first joints of the right thumb and second finger at the lower left corner, the card being face down the tip of your second finger will cover the index. The first joint of your forefinger rests on the opposite corner of the card.

Now if you bend your elbow and wrist inward, till the card almost touches your chest, then throw the card in the air at an angle of about 45 degrees, at the same time giving it a backward spin by a sharp twist of your wrist, as soon as the outward impetus imparted to the card is exhausted, the backward spin will tend to bring it back at the same angle as it mounted. A little practice will enable you to throw the card a few feet and make it return to you, enabling you to catch it at your finger tips. This will be sufficient for you to perform the effect which follows.

You throw a card two or three times and catch it in the manner previously described, then draw your hand back as if to make another throw, leave the card on the top of the pack, then without a moment's hesitation, jerk your arm and wrist forward in exact imitation of the action when you really threw the card. You appear to throw the card to the left front and you open the fingers of the right hand as if the card had just left them, keep your arm extended, forefinger pointing, and slowly turning to the right, you exclaim, "There it goes, right around the room." You follow its imaginary flight with your eyes, gazing intently.

In the mean time, with your left thumb, you pull the card off the pack so that nearly one half of it protrudes to the rear. As your left side comes to the front you bend your right arm inward and extend your left. Keep the back of your left hand to the front and bend the right fingers in toward the palm, then as the left hand passes the right nip the protruding end of the top card with the back of the right fingers in the position of the back hand palm. At once, turn the right hand palm outwards and, extending your left arm to the left, as if indicating where the card now is, exclaim, "There it is."

Drop your left arm and stretching out your right, palm of hand to the front, rapidly produce the card at the finger tips as if you had just caught it in its flight.

The actual transfer of the card from the top of the pack to the back of the right hand is purely a matter of timing and should be practiced before a mirror. If the card and your hands are in the right positions the pick up is instantaneous and imperceptible.

I know of no more effective flourish with cards. It is not difficult, but requires acting, otherwise showmanship. By all means, practice it, and add it to your repertoire.

SERIES No. 2

THE DOUBLE LIFT

No technical description of this sleight, which has come into such great favor of late, has appeared in print, so far as I know. Properly done it is one of the most useful weapons in existence for the card magician. But it must be done correctly, and to clear the way towards an understanding of the right method it may be well to describe the manner in which it is only too often executed, otherwise murdered.

How often do we see a performer fumble with the top cards finally taking hold of two, holding them as if they were made of gold and a crook nearby ready to grab them from him, turn them over on the pack, then face down again, all the while gripping them with all his might, and then push off one card with his thumb and put it in the pack.

Apart from the fact that in the action of taking the cards the performer appeared to be afraid of something, his method of pushing off the single card was entirely different from the way the two cards, supposed to be one only, were taken.

This is all wrong. If you wish to take two cards as one, and have your audience really believe there is one card only, then your actions must be exactly the same as when you take one card. The following method fills these requirements.

While you talking, and looking at your audience, square the deck with your right hand, and, in so doing, lift the inner ends of the two top cards with the ball of the right thumb, pull them a little to the right, as in Fig. 1, and leave them in that position.

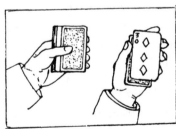

Now, when you call attention to the top card, you bring the tip of the left thumb against the middle of the side of the two cards and push them out, as one card, over the side of the pack. Take them between the tips of the right thumb and first finger, firmly but lightly, in an easy manner, turn them over and place them just above the pack not on it. You hold the left fingers so that the card (s) is received between the ball of the thumb on one side, the first joints of the second and third fingers on the other and the tip of the forefinger rests against the outer end. In this way the two cards are squared perfectly and may be shown freely. (Fig. 2).

Again you take the card (s) by the lower outer corner, between the tips of the right thumb and forefinger, the thumb tip covering the lower index, and turn it (them) face down on the deck. Place the card (s) so that it (they) coincide exactly with the top end of the deck, but do not release the grip of the right thumb and finger. With a slight upward push of the thumb tip on the face of the lower card, release it and draw the top card away to the right.

Although it has taken some time to explain the action it must be understood that the actual movement takes a second only, and there must be no hesitation. The card is turned and at once drawn off the pack smoothly, the lower card being left squarely on the top.

In most cases in which this sleight is used the changed card is immediately inserted in the pack. The action just described brings the card over the side of the pack, with its back to the audience, so that the insertion in the pack follows quite naturally.

Sometimes, however, it is necessary to place the changed card on the table, or face down on the hand of a spectator. To do this, instead of drawing the top card off to the right, as soon as the lower card is released on the top of the pack, you draw the left hand away, the right hand remaining stationary for a moment, then you put the card in the position required.

One very important point should be borne in mind and that is this— whenever you have occasion to turn over the top card to show it to the audience, do it in exactly the same way as when you turn two cards as one.

The perfect way to do this sleight is to push off two cards as one without first separating them from the other cards with the thumb. This is very difficult, but Mr. Dai Vernon, the famous card expert, not only does it, but is able to push off two, three or four cards, as one, at will. By this means he apparently places the top card in the middle of the deck three times in quick succession, each time showing it has returned to the top. In his hands this is one of the most amazing feats possible with cards.

Although this sleight, the double lift, has come into common use in recent years, it is interesting to note that the first mention of it, that I have been able to discover, is in a French book, "Nouvelle Magie Blanche Devoillee," ("New White Magic Revealed"), published in 1853. It appears therein as the first trick with cards, two cards being shown as one, these replaced on the top of the pack, the top card being placed in the middle and then shown as having returned to the top. The author calls it "The Invisible Pass." He claims several tricks that he describes as being his invention.

A NOVEL REVERSE DISCOVERY

EFFECT:—A card having been chosen and returned to the pack, you allow the spectator to shuffle the cards and he then locates his card himself in a surprising way.

METHOD:—A card having been freely chosen, noted, returned to the pack and the pack shuffled, you have secretly brought the card to the top by whatever method you use. You palm the card in your right hand and turn the next one face up to prove that you have not brought the chosen card to the top. Call particular attention to the one turned over and let it be plainly seen that it is a single card, without actually asserting the fact; you may let it drop and pick it up, for instance, then turn it face down again on the top of the deck.

Bring your right hand squarely over the deck, replacing the palmed card on top, and at once turn the pack over to show the bottom card, and spread three or four cards to show it is not near the bottom either.

Turn the cards face down and, while you expatiate on the fact that the chosen card can only be found by having it named and then picked out from the others by running through the whole deck, you get ready for the double lift by separating the two top cards from the rest and pushing them a little off the side of the deck. "However," you say, "there is what we call Fate, Luck, or, if you prefer it, Chance. I have found it a very curious thing that whenever the——of——(you make the double lift and name the face card) is on top of the pack my luck is in. Let's try the experiment. First, will you shuffle the cards?"

You hand the deck to a spectator but you retain the double card in your right hand, face up. Receive the shuffled pack face down on your left hand. Request the spectator to lift up a portion of the deck at the outer end, just a little way, and you insert the double card, face up, at that point. You push it in lengthways until only about an inch of it protrudes, then with the tips of your second and third fingers push the lower card flush with the rest of the cards. The moment you have done this turn the card in the right fingers around to the side of the pack so that its ends protrude on either side.

The position now is that this face up card is in the middle of the pack, in the location chosen by the spectator, its ends extend over the sides of the deck, and under it you have secretly placed the chosen card face up. You ask the spectator who chose the card, to take hold of one end of the deck, while you hold the other. You show that it is impossible to alter the position of the protruding card, unless it is withdrawn and again inserted.

You have the chosen card named and you ask the spectator to lift off the protruding card by its ends, together with all the cards above it. He himself thus reveals his card, face up on the lower portion of the pack, and you remind him that he chose the location, without any interference from you.

INVISIBLE TRANSIT

EFFECT:—Two cards, taken at random, change places at command.

METHOD:—You hand the deck to a spectator and ask him to shuffle the cards thoroughly. You take it back and, while squaring the cards, you separate the two top ones and push them a little sideways in readiness for the double lift. Remarking that you will use the top card, whatever it may be, you turn over two cards as one. Let us suppose that the card that shows is the ten of spades.

"That's a good card for the experiment," you say, as you turn it down and, apparently, lay it face down on the table, really you put down an indifferent card and the ten of spades remains on the top of the pack.

"Let us see what the next card is," you continue, as you square the deck and get ready for another double lift. Again you turn two cards as one, revealing, we will suppose, the six of diamonds. "Excellent. That card makes a fine contrast with the ten of spades. I'll put it over here." You turn the two cards down and, apparently, place the six of diamonds on the other side of the table, this time, of course, it is the ten of spades that you remove and the six of diamonds remains on the top of the pack.

"Remember," you say, "the six of diamonds here," you point to the card just placed down, "and the ten of spades here. I'll replace the ten in its original position on the top of the pack." You pick up the indifferent card first laid on the table, look at it, but be careful not to allow anyone else to get a glimpse of its face, and put it on the top of the pack.

It only remains for you now to order the cards to change places, then turn the two top cards as one, revealing the six of diamonds, and invite a spectator to turn over the card on the table, which proves to be the ten of spades. The feat is not only effective in itself, but will afford excellent practice in the use of the double lift.

THE HAND TO HAND PALM CHANGE

This sleight, which was first described by Prof. Hoffman in "Modern Magic," was devised by Prof. Hellis and it is still the best and simplest method of exchanging one packet of cards for another. It appears to have been lost sight of by modern card workers although some very fine feats are possible by its use. The sleight is not at all difficult and I strongly recommend the reader to use it.

In your left hand you hold palmed, face inward, a packet of cards, A, which is to be changed for another packet, B. With your left side to the front, you take packet B in the same hand, holding it face down by its sides between the thumb and second and third fingers.

As you bring the right hand over to take the packet B, you turn towards the right, palm it, and immediately seize packet A by its sides, carrying it away, slowly and openly. You hold the left hand open for a moment, palm to the front, allowing it to be seen empty, then drop it quietly to your side.

Just before you take away packet A, which was palmed in the left hand, curl your left forefinger up under it and press upwards against the middle of the cards, so taking the bend out of them which was caused by their position in your left hand.

With your right hand you dispose of the exchanged packet A by placing it on the table, handing it to a spectator, or otherwise, as may be necessary for the trick in hand.

The packet now palmed in your right hand is disposed of by adding it to the pack, if this is lying on your table. You simply cover the pack with your hand and draw it back to the edge of the table, so picking it up. If, however, the pack is not available, you await a favorable moment for placing the packet in your pocket under cover of a natural movement, as, for instance, in taking out your handkerchief.

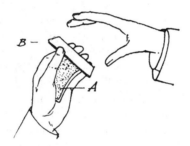

THE HOMING BELLES

This trick utilizes the change, explained on previous page. It has a startling effect and is not at all difficult to do.

EFFECT:—A card is chosen by a spectator. He replaces it and shuffles the pack freely. That card and the three others in the pack of the same value reverse themselves, being found face upward when the deck is spread on the table. These four cards are removed and four other cards are reversed in the deck which is then held by a spectator. The four cards held by the performer return to the pack, in which they are again found to be reversed, and the four cards which were openly turned over in the deck appear in the performer's hand.

METHOD:—Four extra queens, one of each suit, are required. They may be of any pattern as their backs are not seen by the audience. These you have in your left trouser pocket, their faces being inward.

You force one of the four queens of whatever deck you are using; it will enhance the effect if you use a borrowed deck, but be sure to ascertain beforehand that it is complete. You may do this very naturally by running through it to take out the Joker, which you discard for any reason that may occur to you. To force one of four cards is a comparatively easy thing to do, seeing that it makes no difference which one of the four is taken. You allow the spectator to replace his card and at once take the pack and shuffle it freely.

You now have an opportunity to palm the four queens in your left hand. While the spectator is shuffling the pack and you are telling him to make a thorough job of it, not to forget the card he drew, and so on and so forth, you carelessly thrust both hands in your trouser pockets. When he is ready to return the pack, take your right hand out of your pocket and hold it out to receive the cards. Hold the hand so that all can see it is empty. A moment later withdraw your left hand from the left pocket and bring it upwards to meet the right hand. Keep the left hand back outwards till the moment the hands meet, then turn it palm upwards and place the pack face down on the face up queens in its palm. A trial or two before a mirror will give you the correct timing in this action.

The four queens have thus been added to the bottom of the pack faces upward; it is now necessary to distribute them throughout the pack. The best and safest way to do this is by an overhand shuffle. You must remember that the audience must not be allowed to get a glimpse of the bottom of the pack until the four strange queens have been shuffled out of the way.

You turn your right side to the front and you hold the pack so that it is completely shielded by the back of the right hand. To begin the shuffle you run off six or eight cards into the left hand, well down into the fork of the thumb so that the left fingers can be extended over the sides of the cards. Then reaching with them under the pack in the right hand, you pull off the lowest of the queens and at the same time with the left thumb slide the top card of the pack onto it. These two cards fall together on the cards just before shuffled into the left hand. The card pulled off by the thumb hides the face of the reversed queen.

Again run eight or nine cards off the pack into the left hand, then repeat the process of getting a reversed queen off the bottom as already explained. You repeat these movements twice more, with the result that the reversed queens are scattered throughout the deck. A little difficulty may be found in pulling off the bottom cards with the left fingers smoothly, but a very little practice will overcome this. It is much better to shuffle rather slowly and smoothly than to have a series of stops and jerks as the queens are pulled off. It is essential that the cards shuffled off shall go well down into the fork of the thumb.

This process completed, if the pack is one which has a white margin on the back, you may fan the pack and show the faces. The reversed cards will not show up if the fan is spread smoothly, but do not attempt this unless the pack is in good order, and on no account do it if the pack has a solid pattern on the back as with Steamboats. You ask the spectator to name his card and, after announcing what is to take place, you spread the cards face down on the table with a great flourish. Your added queens show up reversed. This is a surprising effect, but you have a more surprising one to follow.

You draw the queens out of the line of other cards towards yourself, still face up, and place them one on top of the other, being careful that they are out of reach of anyone else and that in lifting them you do not expose their backs.

You spread the pack with the faces of the cards towards you and quickly note the four bottom cards. If these do not consist of one card of each suit change whatever cards are necessary to bring this about. You say that you will pick out one card of each suit that you know will give the result you want and that you will reverse these cards in the pack. What you really do is to find the first of the queens belonging to the pack as you run over the faces of the cards. You stop there, calling it by the name of the first of the four bottom cards you noted. You turn this queen face down by pushing it a little off the side of the cards in your left hand and lifting it over with the edge of the packet in your right hand. In this way the queen is turned over sideways towards yourself and no part of its face should have been exposed to the audience.

You find the remaining three queens and repeat the same operation with each, calling them by the names of the other bottom cards, and then reversing them as they lie in the deck. Before you turn the pack face down you slip the left little finger under the four cards whose names you have called, so that you can hold them separated from the rest of the pack. Then having turned the pack down you palm these in your left hand. You hand the pack to a spectator to hold tightly between his hands.

Take the face up queens off the table and place them in your left hand ready for the Hand to Hand Palm Change. You have your left side to the front so that the faces of the cards are towards the audience. You cover them with the right hand as you turn to the left and apparently throw them face down on the table. Really, of course, you make the change and it is the four palmed cards from the pack that fall.

The trick is done and you have only to announce the startling effect that is to take place—the queens to go back home, again reversed, and the four reversed cards to leave the pack and appear in your hand in their place. You have ample opportunity to pocket your four queens, which you have palmed in your right hand, while the pack is examined and the reversed queens are displayed. Then you pick up the four cards from the table and show that they are actually those that just previously were reversed in the deck.

If the reader distrusts his ability to make the change described, a good effect may still be obtained by changing the packets under cover of wrapping the cards in a handkerchief. You throw it over your left hand then in placing the queens under it, palm them, and lift the palmed cards from the left hand. Bring the left hand out and take the cards and the middle of the handkerchief from the above. With the right hand twist the folds of the fabric and hold it thus. This will give you a perfect alibi for keeping the right hand closed and so concealing the cards you hold palmed in it, and, at the finish of the trick, you simply shake the four cards out and thrust the handkerchief into your pocket, at the same time getting rid of the palmed cards.

A BAFFLING SPELL

In this experiment a new and bewildering twist is given to the popular Spelling Bee Trick.

EFFECT:—A spectator takes a card at random from a shuffled pack and lays it aside face down. The deck is again shuffled by a spectator and he selects from it any card he pleases. This card is returned to the pack, which is shuffled and laid on the table. The first card selected is then turned over and, on spelling it in the usual manner, that is, taking a card from the top of the pack for each letter, the second chosen card is revealed on the last letter.

METHOD:—The puzzling part of the feat is that the performer himself does not know the identity of the first card selected until it is turned up, yet the trick is sure fire. The principle on which it rests is this: There are 27 cards in the pack which, with the addition of the word "of" are spelled with either eleven or twelve letters. If, therefore, it is so arranged that the first card is selected from the twenty-seven cards, it will not matter which one is selected and the performer has no need to know it until it is turned over. By placing a card twelfth from the top it will appear on the last letter when a twelve letter card is spelled out and in case of an eleven letter card having been chosen, you have only to say as the card for the last letter is taken, "And the next card is yours," and turn that card over.

The twenty-seven cards are the Ace, two, four, five, six, nine, ten, Jack and King of Hearts and Spades, and all the clubs except the Ace, two, six and ten. If you use this feat as an opener, you can have these cards already on the top of the pack, though it is an easy matter to get them separated openly. You have only to remember, as you run through the pack, professedly to count the cards, to run all the diamonds, the ace, two, six and ten of clubs and the three, seven, eight and Queen of Spades and Hearts to the back of the other cards. Suppose you have done this, as the pack stands, you have twenty-five unsuitable cards on the top followed by the twenty-seven cards from which a selection has to be made.

You run off, by an overhand shuffle, twelve or thirteen cards from the top, thus bringing the suitable cards to the middle portion of the deck. False shuffle several times and place the pack down. Now if you ask a spectator to cut it into two parts, it is practically certain that he will make his cut near the middle. The chance that he cuts anywhere but among the twenty-seven cards, which form the middle portion, is so small that it is negligible. You instruct the spectator to take the top card of the lower part of the pack, after the cut and lay it aside face down, without looking at it himself, or allowing anyone else to see what it is.

You hand the pack to another spectator asking him to shuffle it, then withdraw any card he wishes and return the pack to you. You tell him that you will turn your back for a moment and he is then to hold up his card for all to see. You say you do this because the feat which follows is so extraordinary you wish to avoid all posssibility of him being suspected of having helped you in the denouement.

You turn away and rapidly count off eleven cards from the top and hold the packet of eleven cards separated from the rest of the pack, the thumb holding the division at the back, (you hold the pack by the ends) and the little finger at the front. If you keep your fingers pressed close together this division will be quite invisible from the front. You turn to the audience again and go to the person who chose the card just shown to the spectators. You ask him to replace it in the pack and, holding your left hand under your right, you drop about a quarter of the pack, then several more packets of cards and finally all those under the division made below the eleven cards you counted off. The chosen card is placed on top of this last packet and you drop the eleven cards on it. You do all this openly and keep the fingers of the left hand extended, but do not be tempted to say. "You see I do not insert any of my fingers and I do not hold any break," or anything like that.

Square the pack fairly and slowly, turning it around to show all its sides even, and then place it on the table. Now, having done the trick in reality, it is your cue to impress on the audience the marvellous thing you are going to do. You call attention to the fact that the card now lying face down was chosen at random by a free cut by one of themselves, that you do not know, that nobody can possibly know, what it is, that a second card has been deliberately selected from the pack by another person, and that this has been re-placed at random in the pack. You say you will order this card to place itself in such position in the pack that by spelling out the first card, a card for each letter, it will appear on the last letter, "A manifest impossibility," you say. Then you have the first card chosen turned up. You spell its name, daintly drawing off one card from the top of the deck for each letter. Do this deliber-ately and drop each card separately on the table. If the card proves to be a twelve letter card, when you come to the last letter, you ask the spectator to name the card he chose and then turn the twelfth card dramatically. On the other hand, if it is an eleven letter card, take off the eleventh card and say, "And the very next card is yours. Will you kindly name it?" Then you turn it over with a flourish.

COLOR CHANGES

The term color change is a misnomer since it is applied indifferently to any change of the face card, whether of color, suit or value. Erdnase in his book, "The Expert at the Card Table," uses the term "Transformations" for these moves, but the change was not adopted by the conjuring fraternity and so the designation "Color Change," as is also the case with "Back Palm," is now firmly fixed in magical parlance in spite of the fact that, strictly speak-ing, both are wrong.

The sleight is most effective when the strict interpretation is adhered to, that is, when the change is actually from one color to the other, black to red, or vice versa, and whenever the routine in use allows it, the cards should be so arranged that this will be the case. The value oi the cards to be substituted should also be changed, a ten for an ace, or a picture card for a deuce and so on. However, in many cases the card which is to be used for the change is fixed by chance, and must be taken whether it is a marked contrast or not.

The Color Changes which follow have not, so far as I know, appeared in print. They will be found to be effective and not difficult to do.

No. 1. THE HINGE CHANGE

You hold the pack in the left hand with the first finger doubled back, the nail resting on the back of the rear card. (Fig. 1).

Bring the right hand up to the pack and take it betweeen the tips of the thumb and first fingers, at its lower corners.

Pull back the lower side of the rear card with the tip of the left second finger, so that the card is gripped between the tips of the first and second fingers. (Fig. 2). Pull this card down by moving the left fingers backward slightly, until it just clears the pack at its lower side and at the right angles to it.

The outer side of the card is thus brought to a point near the tips of the right second and third fingers. Push its top outer corner between these two fingers at their top joints, far enough to hold it securely but not allowing it to protrude at the back of the hand. (Fig. 3 and 4).

Show your left hand empty and replace the pack in it, pushing it well into the fork of the thumb, and extending the left fingers flat in front of it.

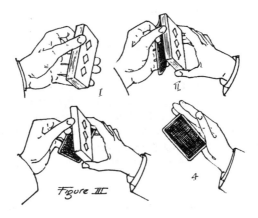

With your right forefinger, extended, point to the face card, bending the second and third fingers a little inward, the back of the hand affording complete cover for the clipped card, which lies out horizontally from the hand.

Bring the right hand in front of the pack, laying the clipped card on the outstretched fingers of the left; the right fingers have, of course, been kept close together up to this point. Place the right middle finger against the outer side of the concealed card and then open the fingers widely, thus allowing the face card of the pack to be seen through the separated fingers.

Suddenly close the fingers of the left hand bringing up the concealed card with them, hinge like, against the face of the deck, and a moment later remove the right hand. The new card appears to simply materialize magically, as there does not appear to be any possible place of concealment for it. This is one of the very best of all the color changes and is well worth the little study required to master it.

No. 2. THE BOOK CHANGE

You hold the pack vertically on its side in the left hand, face card outward, the lower side resting on your outstretched fingers near their roots.

With the right forefinger and thumb grip the lower corners of the deck and carry forward about half the cards to the tips of the left fingers, at the same time allowing several cards to fall forward, face down, behind these cards on to the left fingers. (Fig. 1).

Take these cards with the tips of the thumb and forefinger, by their outer corners, holding them at right angles to, and hidden by, the packet already held by the same digits.

Bend your right hand a little inward toward the body, and call attention to the face card of the packet in the left hand, naming it. (Fig. 2). Replace the right hand in front of the left, again resting the hidden cards on the left fingers and, as you name the card at the face of this portion, you bring the right hand up a little. Under cover of this you close the left fingers, carrying the concealed cards up against the face card of the left hand packet, book fashion, at the same moment you turn the left hand over, bringing the backs of the cards to the front.

Rub the back of the left hand with the cards in your right, then slowly turn the left hand round and show that the change has taken place.

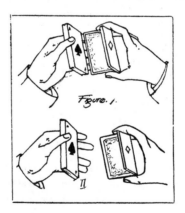

No. 3. A SPECTATOR DOES IT

After showing several changes you assert that the feat is an easy one and that anyone can do it. You ask a spectator if he would like to try.

You say you will pick out an easy card to change and, running through the cards with their faces toward you, you pick out a low red card, say the three of hearts, with a high black card behind it, for instance, the ten of spades. You bring them to the bottom of the pack, the three being the face card.

Call attention to this card, the three of hearts, holding the pack in the left hand, face outwards, thumb on one side and fingers on the other. Take off the two bottom cards, as one, with the right hand, show them to the audience, then replace them, still as one, of course, on the bottom of the pack, but well over the side, as in Fig. No. 1. They are held on the bottom by the pressure of the left thumb, the tips of the second and third fingers rest on the back of the ten of spades.

You ask the spectator to hold out his left hand, palm upward and, apparently you place the three of hearts down on it. To do this you turn your left hand over above his hand and, as you lower it to place the card down, you pull the three of hearts back under the pack with your left thumb, and, with the tips of the second and third fingers, push off the card above it, the ten of spades. (Fig. 2).

At once drop the pack on top of the card now on the spectator's hand. Make him grip the deck with his right hand and rub the face card with his left. Assure him in all seriousness, that if, at the same time he mentally commands the three of hearts to change, it will do so. Then let him turn the pack over and show the change that has taken place. Gently take possession of the pack before he has time to recover from the surprise.

By the "Take or Leave" method, or simply by artful suggestion, you can force the card to which the card is to be changed. This will enhance the effect of the trick.

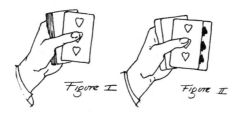

Figure I   Figure II

No. 4. IN REVERSE

This is a novel idea. In order that you may follow the moves clearly it will be well to take a red card, say the seven of hearts, putting it on the face of the deck, and a black card, for example the ace of clubs, which you place under the seven.

You hold the pack in your left hand in the usual position for the color change and stand with your right side to the front. Take the face card off the pack, holding it at the outer end by the tips of the four fingers, pressed close together, and the tip of the thumb at the inner end. Keep the back of your right hand to the audience so that they cannot see any part of the card, but they do see the ace of clubs now on the face of the pack, and you call their particular attention to that card. (Fig. 1).

Now turn your right hand so that the seven of hearts can be seen by everyone and replace it on the ace.

Again take the seven of hearts in your right hand in the same way as before and once more call attention to the ace. Replace the seven on the ace, this time without turning your right hand to show it first, but as you do so, under cover of your right hand, push the ace a little off the side of the pack with the left thumb and carry it away in your right hand by means of the side slip (Fig. 2). Drop your right hand naturally and concentrate your attention on the face card, the seven of hearts.

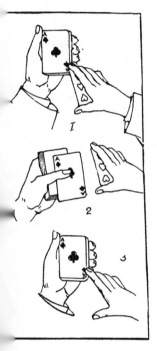

You invite your audience to watch that card very closely, as you are about to show some curious manipulations with it. You bring your right hand over the seven of hearts and imitate exactly the act of taking it off as you did several times before, but really, you leave the palmed ace of clubs on the seven, and then hold your hand as if you held the seven of hearts between the tips of the thumb and fingers. The back of your hand is towards the spectators and, seeing the ace of clubs on the face of the deck, they are naturally satisfied that you have the seven of hearts in your right hand as before (Fig. 3).

Keep your eyes fixed on the imaginary card in your right hand, then suddenly say, "Watch the seven of hearts vanish". You make a tossing motion with your right hand, turning it palm to audience, at the same time making a half turn to the right, imitating the action of back palming a card.

Next turn the hand rapidly to show its back, open the fingers widely, then press them together and again turn it to show the palm. In fact, you make all the regular moves which pertain to the back and front palm, and, having no card to conceal, you are able to do them cleanly, to say the least.

In the meantime your left hand has not been idle. You drop it to your side, push the face card, the ace of clubs, down against the side of your leg, hold it there for a moment with the tips of your fingers, while you pull the pack upwards, holding it in the fork of the thumb until the outer edge of the ace clears the pack, then slide the pack down under it, thus transferring the ace to the back of the deck. This will cause the seven of hearts to become the face card and you must, of course, be careful to hold the pack with its face towards your body, so that the spectators cannot get a glimpse of the seven of hearts.

In the course of your manipulations with the imaginary card you bring your right hand with its back to the audience, close the fingers and turn the hand around. Pretend to crumple the card to pieces, then slowly open the fingers and show all parts of the hand. The card has vanished, as you promised it would.

"The fragments of the card are floating around," you say, "and I can reassemble them. Watch."

You make a catch in the air and bring your right hand down on the face of the deck with a slap and, as you remove it the audience see the seven of hearts back again. You must be very careful to hold the deck with its back to the front until you make the slap.

The effect of this little comedy with cards can only be realized by actually working it before an audience. There is a minimum of sleight of hand in it but plenty of scope for acting.

No. 5. SOME PATTER SUGGESTIONS

The color change is most often used as a mere flourish but it can also be effectively employed as an introduction to a series of card tricks or as an interlude between set tricks. For instance, let us say you have the following cards on the top of the deck, Jack of Hearts, Queen of Hearts, Three of Diamonds, Ten of Clubs and Ace of Spades; the Jack being the top card and the others following it in the order given.

To illustrate the use to which playing cards can be put to add color to a story, you recite the following verse, changing the face card of the pack by varying color change sleights at the appropriate word:

> The young man (J. H.) makes of Hearts (Q. H.) his trumps,
> Then Diamonds (3 D.) he plays,
> But when his dream romantic slumps,
> Too oft to Clubs (10 C.) he strays,
> With varying luck the game is played,
> The final trick goes to a Spade (A. S.).

Here is another and more ambitious example of patter to be illustrated by the use of the color change:

Once upon a time a QUEEN'S HEART was WON by a KING. He had a large DIAMOND which cost lots of JACK. People at the wedding saw a great PAIR. One night, however, the KING played the DEUCE by coming home to the pal-ACE at THREE-SEVEN A. M. This made the QUEEN SICK, so she seized a CLUB from a TRAY and THREATENED to beat him up. Be-FORE she could strike him the KING tried TRUMPS, handing her FOUR TENS, remarking, "Here, do some shopping with what I WON." So they lived happily ever after and no SPADES were needed.

It should be a pleasant diversion for the enthusiast to arrange the various moves whereby the change can be made to best advantage with the color changes he has mastered. The four tens might be crimped and at the right time secretly pushed from the back into the right hand and then produced in a fan from the knee.

CARDS FROM THE AIR

THE BEST FRONT HAND PRODUCTION

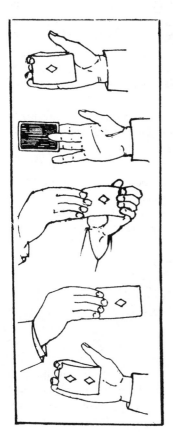

The following method of apparently catching cards from the air is the invention of an amateur magician of Wellington, N. Z. It is, I think, the best sleight for the purpose that has as yet been evolved in that the hand can be freely shown from all sides in the action. This is not possible with other methods.

You have about ten cards palmed in your right hand in the usual way. Bend the top joint of your second finger under the top edge of the palmed cards (Fig. 1), then as you make a catching motion in the air, stretching out your arm, you straighten the fingers sharply. This causes the packet to fly out from the palm into view at the finger tips. (Fig. 2) The cards are held securely and squarely together as one card, by the top joints of the first and third fingers on the face of the card, and of the second finger at the back.

The moment the card is produced at the finger tips you press your thumb tip on the back of the packet at the corner immediately behind the tip of the first finger, and bend the other three fingers into the palm. The impression to be made on the spectators is that of having caught a card at the tips of the finger and thumb.

You show the card (s), turning the hand to show the palm empty, then with the left hand take hold of the outer end of the packet and bend the cards sharply back into the right hand, where they are again palmed, with the exception of the front card, which is stripped off by the left thumb and fingers and held up to view. (Fig. 3).

The right hand drops naturally and you are ready to repeat the catching of a card; you continue the movements until your supply of cards is exhausted. During the action you have your right side to the front. Vary the point at which the card is caught as much as you can and always see the card in the air yourself before you catch it.

FRONT HAND PRODUCTION. No. 2

For this production the cards must be palmed with their faces inward, that is next to your palm.

With about a dozen cards palmed in this manner you bend the fingers inward until you are able to pull down the top end of the outermost card as in Fig. 1. Your arm is bent so that the hand is about six inches away from the body.

You release the card by straightening the thumb and the card will fly out from the rest, at the same moment you jerk your arm forward and catch the card by its inner end at the tips of the thumb and fingers. (Fig. 2). With practice it will be found that the cards can be caught at their extreme ends so that practically the whole card is in view at the finger tips. Success in this sleight is mainly a matter of timing the release of the card and the forward jerk of the arm.

The sleight can be done very rapidly and it is one of the few moves which gain in effect by being done quickly. Some performers beginning the action with about twenty cards palmed, catch a dozen or so at the finger tips singly, and then suddenly produce all the others fanned out. (Fig. 3). It is well to begin with not more than eight or ten cards.

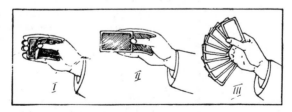

This sleight can be used to good advantage in the production of the full pack as a preliminary to a series of flourishes. You have the rest of the pack in a clip on your hip, or in your lower vest pocket. After producing say, five or six cards, you turn a little more to the left, reach out with your right hand as far as possible and produce the last of the palmed cards in a fan. At the same moment with your left hand grip the rest of the pack from the clip or pocket, adding them to the cards already in your left hand.

Turn now to face thhe audience, place the cards just caught on top of the pack, and, as you do so, push a good load of cards from the back of the pack with your left forefinger into the right palm. Riffle the cards in the left hand and produce the palmed cards from the left knee fanned out to fullest extent. Add these cards to the others in your left hand and proceed to your flourishes such as —

THE ARM SPREADS

No. 1. THE SPREAD AND TURN-OVER

This flourish is the basis of all the spreads which follow and should be mastered before the others are attempted. It is not difficult but, as with all good sleights, practice is necessary.

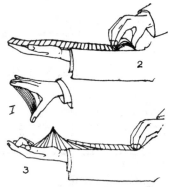

You hold the pack in the right hand in the position for springing the cards from hand to hand. (Fig. 1). Extend the left arm straight out, level with your shoulder, the palm of the hand being uppermost, and your right side to the front.

With the right hand spring the cards along the left arm from the finger tips to the elbow, the first card overlapping the tips of the fingers about an inch. (Fig. 2). Close the left fingers under the first card of the line and so cause all the cards to reverse in turn. The arm must be kept straight and rigid and the cards should be in a direct line. (Fig. 3).

VARIATIONS FOR FINISHING THIS SLEIGHT

a. Simply drop the left arm to the side, so that the cards fall cleanly into the left hand after the turn-over.

b. In reversing the cards, instead of allowing them to fall on the arm, they drop into the right hand, which is held a little below the left elbow. To make them drop in this fashion you must turn the left forearm slightly inward at the moment that the cards are turned over. They should drop very prettily like a cascade.

c. After the cards have been turned over and lie face up on the left arm, insert your right thumb under the cards nearest the elbow, turn it upward and then press it downward, towards the left wrist, thus causing all the cards to turn over again. Finish by dropping the left arm and catching the cards in the left hand as they slide down.

No. 2. THE GLIDE

To execute this flourish you hold the deck between the right thumb and second finger at diagonally opposite corners. (Fig. 1). Spring the cards along the arm from the fingertips in the usual way, but with the faces outwards. (Fig. 2).

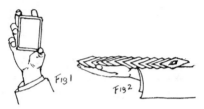

Then drop the left arm, at the same time moving it a little inward, causing the cards to slide down the arm into the left hand. This is one of the prettiest of the arm spreads.

No. 3. THE BACK ARM REVERSE

You stand with your left side to the front. Spring the cards along the back of your left arm, starting at the knuckles of your hand, and bringing the last card to a point about two inches from your elbow. (Fig. 1).

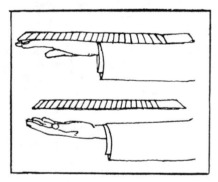

Hold the left arm rigid and lower your whole body by bending your knees, then straighten up and when the arm reaches its former elevation drop it a little and quickly turn it over, bringing the palm upwards. (Fig. 2).

Catch the cards as they fall, on this side of the arm, which should be dropped slightly as the cards land. This helps to prevent the cards being disarranged as they land on the arm.

No. 4. THE UPRIGHT SPREAD

For this particular flourish, which has a surprising effect, you hold the pack upright in the right hand, face outwards. The thumb at the middle of one side, the fingers on the other side. (Fig. 1).

With your left arm outstretched, back of the hand to the front and held vertically, you place the pack against the left palm. Spring the cards along the inside of the arm. (Fig. 2).

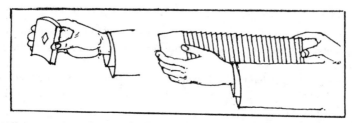

Bend the left fingers and grip the first cards of the row tightly against the palm of your hand, and with the right fingers, at the opposite end of the line of cards and stretched out as far as possible, press the cards under them firmly against the side of your arm. As much as possible of the faces of the cards should show above the arm.

No. 5. THE ELBOW CATCH

You spread the cards on the left arm as in No. 1, then you turn the whole line of cards over by bending the second and third fingers inward.

With a sharp upward jerk of the arm you cause the cards to slide back and downward, catching them in a bunch at the elbow by bending the forearm back quickly.

From this position you toss the pack upward by extending the forearm and jerking the arm upward. Catch the pack on the back of the hand.

No. 6. THE TURN-OVER AND RIGHT HAND CATCH

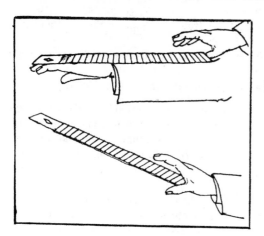

You spread the cards on the left arm as in No. 1, and turn them over as described. Put your right hand at the elbow and, as the last card turns over, insert your thumb under it, the hand being palm outwards. (Fig. 1).

With the left arm make a slight upward motion, and then drop it to your side sharply. At the same moment you lunge forward with your right hand and catch the whole line of cards between the thumb and the fingers. (Fig. 2).

The fact that the cards overlap one another, and that the right thumb is then below the bottom card, makes it a comparatively easy feat to gather them all. This flourish may be effectively repeated by spreading the cards on the right arm and then catching them in the left hand.

No. 7. THE BACK ARM CATCH

You stand facing the audience, the left forearm bent horizontally in front of the body. Spring the cards along the forearm from the tips of the fingers to the elbow.

Place your right hand to the rear of the last card near the elbow, inserting the first joints of the fingers under that card, the palm of the hand being to the front.

With the left arm make a short upward swing, then drop it sharply to your side, at the same moment sweep the right hand quickly outwards in a circular direction from left to right, and catch the cards in the action.

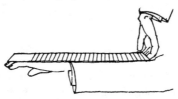

No. 8. VANISH OF PACK

You proceed as in No. 7, catching the pack as described. Continue the movement of your right arm behind your back, and, turning your left side to the front, thrust the cards into the left armpit at the back, at once pressing the left arm to your side.

Turn to the front again and bring your right hand into view, as if still holding the cards in it, and make a tossing motion, simulating the action of throwing the cards into the air. Concentrate your gaze on the hand and then look up as if watching the cards disappear.

After a moment or two lift the left arm and let the cards fall into the right hand.

No. 9. THE HALF TURN-OVER AND CATCH

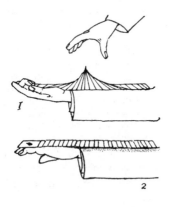

To begin with you spring the cards on the left forearm as in No. 1, from the finger tips to the elbow. Bend the second and third fingers inward and turn the first cards over until the cards in the middle of the line are erect.

Place the right hand over the upright cards at the middle of the line, the back of the hand being upward and the fingers ready to close against the thumb.

Hold your left arm rigid and lower the whole body by bending your knees, then straighten up and when the arm reaches its former height, drop it and catch the cards between the thumb and fingers by their upper ends. It will be found that by this procedure, the cards remain in position in the air for just the moment necessary to make a successful catch.

The usual method of doing this flourish is to jerk the left arm upwards then drop it sharply to the side, the right hand making a quick lunge and catching the cards. The much better method described above was given to me and demonstrated by Mr. John Mulholland in whose hands it became the acme of ease and grace.

No. 10. THE ONE HAND CATCH

For this difficult flourish you stand facing the audience. Hold your right forearm, elbow bent, horizontally in front of the body. With the left hand spread the cards on the back of the right forearm, starting at the finger tips, the first few cards overlapping them to the front, and extending the line of cards for not more than twelve inches.

Turn to the left with a slight upward jerk of the arm leave the cards in the air, bring the right arm back and up sharply, and with a quick forward lunge catch the cards, the thumb being under them and the fingers on top.

An elaboration of the flourish is to divide the pack, spreading one-half on the right arm and the other half on the left. Both portions are then thrown into the air simultaneously and so caught. A brilliant effect that will require some practice.

No. 11. THE HAT CATCH

For this flourish you wear your hat, silk hat for preference.

Holding the cards in the usual way you spread them on the back of your left arm. (Fig. 1). Grasp the brim of your hat with your right hand, then

Figure 1.   Figure 2

jerk the line of cards upwards by quickly raising your left arm, immediately afterwards dropping it to your side.

Swing the hat around in front of you with a circular motion and sweep the cards into it before they fall. (Fig. 2).

By having a bag fake in the hat it could be so fixed that the cards would fall to the bottom but would be prevented from falling out. After catching the cards in the hat, turn it crown up and shake it, but the cards do not fall. In the meantime you have had ample opportunity to secure another pack from a clip on your left hip. Turn the hat mouth upwards and produce this pack from the crown in a fan.

If a hat is worn for your entrance this would make a brilliant opening for a series of manipulations.

No. 12. THE DOUBLE SPREAD

Divide the pack as nearly in half as possible and riffle shuffle the two portions together, letting the cards fall card for card from each packet alternately. Place this elongated pack face up across the palm of your left hand, holding it between the thumb and fingers of your right hand at the point of intersection of the two packets.

Squeeze the cards firmly between the right thumb and fingers bending them a little, then spring them along the forearm, nearly to the elbow. Turn the whole line over by bending the left fingers inward, exactly as in turning a single line of cards.

Insert the right thumb under the cards nearest the elbow as they turn, jerk the forearm sharply up, then drop it to your side, and catch the double line of cards in the right hand. The movements are practically the same as in the single line flourish.

A ROUTINE FOR ARM SPREADS

With a view to helping the reader to arrange a series of arm spreads and catches the following is taken from that classical work on Card Magic, "The Art of Magic." The manipulations that follow are those adopted by Mr. J. N. Hilliard, the editor.

    a. Left arm spread, toss and catch.
    b. Right arm spread, toss and catch.
    c. Spread on right arm, catch in right hand.
    d. Spread on right arm, toss and catch the line of cards on the opposite side of the arm.
    e. Turn the line over, toss into the air and catch in the right hand.

The five movements should follow one another quickly, the time taken up being about twenty seconds.

The student should thoroughly master No. 1 Spread before attempting any of the other sleights. With this at his finger tips the rest of the flourishes will give him little trouble.

SERIES 3

Card Manipulations No. 3

By JEAN HUGARD

TRICKS

THE MAGICAL PRODUCTION OF
A PACK OF CARDS

This is a logical opening for a series of feats with cards. You prepare by placing the deck in your lower left vest pocket, one end protruding so that you can readily take hold of it. If necessary push a silk handkerchief into the pocket first.

To begin you show a large silk foulard, you shake it out and turn it around, then, holding one corner in your teeth and the opposite corner in your left hand, you stretch the silk out so that your vest is covered. You thrust your right hand under the silk, pushing out its center, which you seize with your left hand. Turn this hand over quickly, causing the silk to fall down over it, and revealing— nothing. So you try again.

You stretch the silk out as before and again thrust your right hand behind it. This time you seize the deck, pull it out of the vest pocket and thrust one corner against the middle of the silk. You let the corners of the silk drop and quickly grasp the pack through the silk from the outside with your left hand. Turn this hand so that the silk falls over it, exposing the cards which you at once fan the fullest possible extent.

Fig. 1

THE CARDINI SNAP
COLOR CHANGE

You hold the pack in your left hand, face outwards,, almost upright. Insert the top joint of the third finger under the face card, the tips of the other three fingers resting on its outer side. Bend the card up lengthwise slightly by squeezing it between the thumb and fingers. Fig. 2.

Call attention to the face card by snapping it several times with the nail of the right second finger. At the very moment that you snap the card a third time, sharply extend the left fingers, carrying away the face card, so that its free side strikes against the right hand at the middle of the inner side of the right forefinger.

Fig. 2

Pressing the right hand downwards you bend the card in half lengthwise, and at the same instant grasp the pack by its outer corners between the thumb and forefinger. The second and third fingers are extended, being kept close to the forefinger, and the little finger is also stretched out but held separate from the others. The second card of the deck is thus exposed (Fig. 3), while the first card is hidden by the three fingers of the right hand, left fingers retaining their grip of the card.

Under cover of the surprise caused by the change, a moment later you move the hands backward and upward a little, as if to show the new card to better advantage, and bending the left fingers inward you bring the first card back under the pack. The move is hidden by the back of the right hand which lifts the pack slightly to allow the card to pass. Complete the action by running the thumb and fingers along the ends of the cards, squaring them, then casually show the right hand empty.

The change is instantaneous. I am indebted to the Ace of manipulators, Cardini, for this fine addition to the standard color changes.

Fig. 3

Fig. 4

NEW PALM OF TOP CARD AND A COLOR CHANGE

You have pack in your left hand. You bring your right hand over to take the deck, holding the hand vertically with its back to the audience. As the hand arrives at the deck, with the left thumb push the top card halfway off to the right, letting it strike against the right forefinger, but holding the left side of this card firmly on the deck; continue the movement of the right hand and grasp the pack between the thumb at the rear end and the two middle fingers at the outer end. The top card is thus doubled over lengthwise and you can then turn the pack upright with its face to the front in perfect safety. Practically the whole of the palm is visible to the audience. You replace the pack in the left hand, as that hand moves away the bent card springs automatically against the right palm.

To apply this sleight to an effective COLOR CHANGE you take the pack in right hand, bending the top card as described above. Hold the deck up, displaying the face card and naming it, turn to the left, transferring pack to left hand and palming the bent card in right. Turn the pack over in left hand bringing its face to the onlookers. Point to the bottom card with the right forefinger, then slowly pass the right hand over it, leaving the palmed card on the face of the deck. The change is made.

THE AMBITIOUS CARD

The trick known by this name has long been a favorite. There are few card men who do not include a version of it in their repertoire. Briefly the plot of the trick is that a chosen card appears on the top of the deck, the place of honor, and although it is repeatedly placed in the middle it constantly returns to the top. I am giving here a new and convincing move and a startling finish.

After the card has been shown by the usual methods to have returned to the top several times, you turn the card over on the top to show it and turn it face down again. Take the pack in your right hand, fingers at the outer end, thumb at the inner. Lift the pack and turn it, calling attention to the bottom card and naming it. Turn the pack face down and replace it on the palm of the left hand, but as you do so palm the top card by the One Hand Top Palm, (C. M. No. 1, p. 2).

With the same hand cut off about half the pack and hold this half, A, a couple of inches to the right of the packet in the left hand, B. With the left thumb pull off the top card from A on to the top of B. The onlookers naturally take this to be the chosen card and you so refer to it. You draw off several more cards on to B, in fact any number that may be called for, then drop the rest of the cards in the right hand on top of those in your left. Lift the deck with your right hand, adding the palmed card to the top, turn the deck face up showing the bottom card still in place. Riffle the cards, turn and show the top card. The Ambitious Card is back.

The climax to the trick that follows is daring but highly effective. Beforehand you have fixed small pellets of good adhesive wax to the two lower buttons of your vest. It is well to have two in case one is knocked off accidentlly. You take the card from the top of the pack in your right hand and as you discourse on the impossibility of keeping a good man down, and so on, you get the wax pellet off the vest button and press it on the back of the top card. You put the card in your right hand on the floor apparently, really you make the bottom change and it is the card with the wax pellet on its back that drops face down and the Ambitious Card is left on the bottom of the pack. You place your right foot squarely on the floor card, being careful to cover it. At the same time you quietly slip the Ambitious Card from the bottom to the top by the Side Slip sleight.

You impress on the audience that you have put a stopper on the pack by your favorite method. (See Hindu Shuffle C. M. 2). You step back, the card has gone. Incredulous you turn the top card, The Ambitious Card is home again.

You take the first opportunity of removing the card from the sole of your shoe, being careful in the meantime not to walk with your back to the audience.

RISING CARD

THE HOROWITZ THUMB METHOD

You bring the card, or cards, which are to rise, to the top of the pack by your favorite method. (See Hindu Shuffle, C. M. 2). You then fan the deck, not too widely, in the left hand, with the inner end well down in the crotch of the thumb. At the moment the fan is completed, push the top card down a little with your right thumb and then move its top end an inch or so to the left, so that the card is upright instead of inclining to the right.

Move the left little finger behind the fan of cards and hold the cards between the three other fingers in front and the little finger at the rear, leaving the thumb free.

You put the tip of left thumb on the middle of the lower end of the card just straightened and push it slowly upwards until it projects as far as possible, without exposing any part of the thumb, above the edges of the fanned cards. By moving the thumb towards the left you make the card travel along the edge of the fan with almost its full face in view. (Fig. 5).

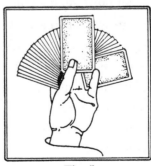

Fig. 5

When the card reaches the left side of the fan, pull it down about half its length and push its right side in amongst the other cards. Close the fan with your right hand and leave the card projecting from the deck. Square the cards and, taking the pack by its inner end, hold it out to the spectator, allowing him to remove his card. False shuffle and repeat with the other cards.

This effective impromptu trick was originated by Mr. Sam Horowitz. A version of it appeared in a magical journal recently with apparent credit to another magician. I am glad to be able to give the correct working by permission of Mr. Horowitz.

THE BROADWAY RISE

A NEW IMPROMPTU RISING CARD EFFECT

EFFECT:—The pack is held facing the audience in a vertical position, its sides parellel with the floor, by the lower corners between the left thumb and forefinger. A card previously chosen and returned, rises lengthways, having apparently made a half turn sideways in the pack.

METHOD:—A card having been chosen by a spectator, it is returned to the pack, brought to the top by the Hindu Shuffle and palmed in the right hand by the One Hand Top Palm (see C. M. pp. 2). This done you take the pack by the sides between the tips of the right fingers and thumb, the fingers pressed closely together being on the side nearest the audience.

Making a pretense of trying to cut at the chosen card, with your left hand pull off a few cards from the top of the pack, and turn them face up. The card thus exposed is not, of course, the chosen card so you replace the packet on top of the pack in the right hand. In doing so you insert the tip of the left forefinger between the palmed card and the right forefinger, pushing its middle downwards, so that instead of being bent up into the right hand it is bent down away from the hand, leaving a space between the card and the fingers.

With the left hand pull out a second packet, turning it up and showing its bottom card, again a wrong one. Replace this packet on top of the palmed card, which will thus be held lengthwise between the halves of the pack. Take the pack from below in the left hand between the thumb and tip of first finger holding it with sides parallel to the floor, cards upright and bottom card squarely to the front. The left hand hides the part of the card which projects at the lower side of the pack.

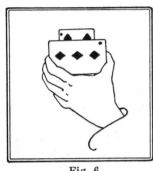

Fig. 6

With the right fingers square the upper side of the deck preventing the end of the chosen card from projecting. This card is now made to rise by an upward pressure of the little finger at the middle of its lower end, the right hand being waved over the upper side of the deck as if controlling the rising card (Fig. 6). When the card has been pushed up as far as it will go the right thumb and little finger, pressing on its sides, raise it quickly to full length, immediately afterwards taking it by the upper end between the tips of the thumb and forefinger.

A RISING CARD COMEDY

Any deck is shuffled by a spectator. You allow a card to be freely selected, have it returned to the pack and you control it, bringing it to the top. You false shuffle, retaining the card on the top. You then hold the cards in your left hand as in Fig. 7, the back of the pack being towards your body.

Making a pretense of taking a pellet of soap from your vest button you feint to stick it on the lower right hand corner of a card. You then see a lady's hair on some gentleman's coat and you go through the motion of plucking it off and sticking it by one end to the imaginary pellet of soap at the back of the pack.

In all seriousness you call attention to the hair, which you say everyone can see hanging down from the deck, and you pretend to take the free end between your right thumb and first finger. You move your right hand in circular fashion outward and upward, keeping it exactly the same distance from the pack as if a hair were really there. As your right hand comes up over the pack, push your left thumb upwards, twisting the top card into view as if it were being slowly pulled upwards. (Fig. 8.)

The movement of the right hand and the card must synchronize, the movement of the card must be just as if it were actually pulled upward by a hair. (Fig. 8.) Finally pretend to remove the soap and the hair from the top right hand corner of the card and toss the card out to the audience.

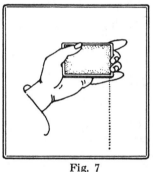
Fig. 7

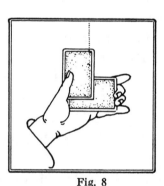
Fig. 8

AN UNWITTING WIZARD

Any deck may be used. You have the cards shuffled by a spectator and then cut into two packets about equal. Your victim chooses which packet shall be used in the trick and the other you put in your outside coat pocket on the right hand side. You take the remaining packet and allow the spectator to make free choice of one card. It is replaced and you bring it to the top by your favorite method. You hand the pack to be shuffled and in so doing you palm the top card by the One Hand Top Palm. (C. M. No. 1, p. 2.)

As he begins to shuffle you say you will take one card from those in your pocket and with it as an indicator you will try to find the chosen card. You put your hand in your pocket and you bring out the palmed card, face downwards, of course. You thrust this card into the cards held by the spectator, but the card at that point is not the selected card. You try again and again you fail. You hand the card to the spectator and ask him to make the third attempt. But he also fails to locate his card.

You ask him to name the card and then suggest that he may succeed if the indicator card is held face up. He will be surprised to find that the card he holds is the card he selected. It will be noted that the working of the trick is extremely simple, yet with proper acting the performer will find the resulting mystery and amusement a rich return for little trouble.

THE RADIO CARDS

A favorite trick with generations of magicians has been the invisible passage of cards from one packet to another. It dates at least as far back as the early part of last century and was used by the great Robert Houdin himself. He says in his book, "Secrets of Magic and Conjuring": "This is a trick which I can specially recommend to conjurers as producing an extraordinary illusion. The modifications I have made in it give it an entirely new effect." In recent years a very great improvement in the feat has been made, the spectators being allowed to select any three cards amongst those in the first packet. At the close of the experiment these three cards are found to have passed to the other packet.

This method entails the use of duplicate sets of cards, a switch of envelopes and preparation. The very latest form of the trick does away with these aids and brings it into the category of the best and most favored card feats, those that can be done with any pack, at any time or place, by anyone who has acquired the necessary skill. There is no preparation.

You invite a spectator to assist you. You have him shuffle a deck of cards and then count off twelve, face down, on a table to your left. You instruct him to take the twelve cards to the audience and have three cards taken out, noted, marked and then returned to the packet which he is to shuffle, and bring back to you. While this is being done and in going to put it on a table to your right, you palm nine cards in your left hand from the bottom of the pack. The remainder of the cards you place face down to the right of the glass.

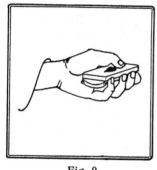

Your volunteer assistant having done his work brings his packet back to you. You take it in your right hand, letting it be seen that your hand is empty as you take the cards. You place the cards in your left hand, holding them between the tips of the fingers on one side and the thumb on the other, so that the packet hides the nine cards you have palmed in that hand.

Fig. 9

(Fig. 9.) With the cards held in this manner you can gesticulate with perfect freedom and there can be no suspicion that you hold anything but the visible twelve cards.

With your right hand lift the glass and show it, put it down a little to the left of the remainder of the deck, and take the cards from the left hand, executing the Hand to Hand Palm Change (C. M. No. 2, p. 25). Drop the nine cards into the glass, faces outwards. With your left hand gesture towards glass showing the hand empty and with the right hand draw the pack off the table, adding the palmed cards to it.

As you take the pack to your assistant who should now be on the left of your other table, palm three cards from the bottom in your left hand. You drop the pack on the table and ask him to again count off twelve cards, FACE DOWN. These of course, are the same twelve cards that he originally dealt and the three marked cards are amongst them, so that the transfer has been made before the audience know what you are going to do. As soon as he has placed twelve cards on the table you call attention to the fact that these twelve cards plus the twelve in the glass make 24 so that he should have 28 cards left in his hands. As he verifies this you casually pick up the twelve cards letting your hand be seen to be empty and lay them face down on the three cards palmed in your left hand. This action should be tried out before a mirror. You bring your left hand up about waist high, its back to the audience, and as the right hand is brought down to meet it, the moment the hands come together, you turn the left hand palm upwards and put the twelve cards on it.

As soon as the assistant has counted the 28 cards, have him put them in his pocket and then take the packet of twelve cards off your left hand which you have held out flat right under his eyes, and grip them firmly between his two hands. The trick is done. You use whatever form of hocus-pocus to account for the flight of the cards to work up the effect. (An ancient magical spell is given below for those who can use such things . . . . it may raise the Devil, I don't know, I have never tried it.)

Finally you take the cards from the glass, holding them very openly, count them one by one, calling their names and letting them drop on the table. (See the Flourish Count, p. 72.) There are nine cards only and the three selected cards are not amongst them. Your assistant counts his cards, he has fifteen and amongst them are the three marked cards. While the actual working of the trick is simple, there are only two moves to cover, with good presentation it is one of the most striking of all card feats that can be done without any preparation.

The following incantation is from "The Tragical History of Dr. Faustus" by Christopher Marlowe. If the reader is interested in the application of magical effects to stage work he will find in this play the illusion of pulling off a man's leg and its restoration. The play was written in 1604.

"Sint mihi Dei Acherontis propitii: Valet nomen triplex Jehovae Ignei aerii: aquatani spiritus salveti: Orientis princeps Beelzebub: Inferni ardentis monarcha et Demagorgon, propitiamus vos, ut appareat Mephistophilis, quod tumeraris per Jehovam, Gehennum et Consecration aquam, quam nunc spargo signnum sue crucis quod nunc facis, et per vota nostra, ipse nunc spurgat nobis dictatis Mephistophilis."

If the cards don't fly after that, well......

THE VOR-AC(E)-IOUS MAGICIAN

EFFECT: The aces are laid in a row, three cards are dealt on each of them. The aces vanish and are found in a spectator's pocket.

METHOD: Any pack may be used. First run through it casually and arrange that no ace lies amongst the top or bottom half-a-dozen cards. Then holding the pack face down in the left hand you slip the tip of your little finger above the four bottom cards. You push the rest of the pack forward about an inch, take the outer end of the pack between right thumb above, the fingers below, and turn it over lengthwise towards yourself. The four cards separated by the little finger will remain face downward on the left hand. A slight movement of the hands as the turn is made will cover the retention of these cards. (Fig. 10 and 11.)

You advance to a spectator with the deck lying face down on your left hand. You spread the cards slowly and ask him to take out the aces as you come to them. As soon as the fourth ace has been removed you turn the pack again lengthwise but this time you take it by the inner end and lift it outwards to an upright position. The

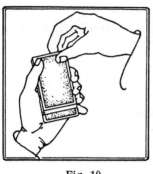

Fig. 10   Fig. 11

four face cards are now towards you and you slip the tip of your little finger below them.

Still holding the pack upright you take an ace from the person holding them, put it face up on top of the deck, and as soon as it covers the top reversed card, you drop the pack to a horizontal position, showing it, and count "One". Take the next ace and put it on the first, counting "Two". Treat the next two aces in the same way. There are now eight cards face up on the top of the deck, the audience knowing only of the four aces, and you have the eight cards separated from the rest by the tip of your little finger. You turn these eight cards face down. Do this naturally without haste but without hesitation. The extra cards will never be noticed.

Deal off the four top cards in a row face down, calling them aces. You say you are about to make four heaps of four cards and you count off **sixteen** cards, one on top of the other, into your right hand, pushing them well down into the crotch of the thumb so that the faces of the first four cards, the aces, are not exposed. You deal three cards on top of each supposed ace. This leaves you with four cards over and you suddenly discover that you made a mistake, you needed twelve cards, not sixteen, but you have thus got the aces where you want them. Being careful not to expose their faces you drop them on top of the pack, which you then pick up and in squaring it. you slip the tip of your left little finger under the top five cards. An easy matter if you drop the four cards a little over the side of the rest.

You palm these five cards in your right hand as you go to a spectator on your left. You hand him the pack, telling him to run through it, satisfy himself that there are no more aces in it and then hold it tightly between both hands. As he runs over the cards you suddenly thrust your right hand into his inside coat pocket and bring out the indifferent card at the tips of your fingers, leaving the aces behind. You accuse him of trying to play a trick on you, and, if he is a good subject, he will promptly button up his coat as you whisper to him to do that, "Just to make them laugh."

Returning to the packets on the table, you take them up, one on top of the other, being careful not to expose the bottom cards. As you put the first packet on your left hand you slip your little finger on it and as the last packet is placed on the others you can palm the bottom four smoothly, by the bottom palm in the left hand. Then holding the remaining cards in your right hand, with the left you take your handkerchief from your pocket as if to wrap the cards in it, but you change your mind and give them to another person to hold. You order the aces to fly from his hand and return to the pack.

The cards are counted, there are twelve only and the aces are not amongst them. The spectator who holds the pack is told to take the aces out. There are none there. You are surprised, taken aback, dumfounded. (Vas you dere, Sharlie?) Then you recall that you sent them with a little more force than was necessary, and you ask him to search his pockets. Finally he unbuttons his coat and finds the four aces in his inside coat pocket. Their insertion took place so early in the trick that the spectator himself is quite likely to have forgotten that you went to his pocket to take out a card, while to the audience this climax will come as a startling surprise.

THE RED AND THE BLACK

False shuffling is a weak point with many card handlers and this trick is strongly recommended for use in remedying this defect. You separate the red cards from the black and you show all the red cards at the top and all the black cards below them. You shuffle the cards thoroughly, but at command the colors separate, the black and red being shown all together as before.

You take any pack and openly separate the red cards from the black by alternately pushing the red cards up and the black cards down, and then stripping them apart. (C. M. No. 1, p. 10). Put the reds on the blacks and spread the pack showing the separation. Holding the pack in readiness for an overhand shuffle, with your right thumb pull back about half the black cards, making a break between them and the rest of the pack and retain the break. With the tip of your left thumb divide about half the reds from the others. Retain these cards in your left hand by keeping the thumb tip on them and raise the rest of the pack as in the first move of an overhand shuffle.

Drop the cards above the break held by the right thumb, about half the deck, on top of the packet in the left hand; again raise the right hand and drop the remaining cards on those in the left hand. If you now run over the faces of the cards you will find that their order is black, red, black, red, and that each section consists of about one quarter of the deck. This order must be kept in the course of various false shuffles.

First use the standard false shuffle, packets being apparently dropped alternately on each side of the first packet dropped into the left hand, really they will all go behind. Do this twice and follow it with the Hunter False Shuffle. You undercut half the deck and rapidly draw off six cards from the right hand packet on top of the left hand cards, with the left thumb one by one. Drop the remainder on top but about half an inch in front. Pick up the lower half, on which the six cards have just been run, the step allowing this to be done cleanly, and again shuffle off the same six cards one by one, finally dropping the remaining cards on top. This shuffle simply reverses the order of six cards in the first movement, while the second movement replaces them in the original order. The shuffle is most deceptive and so easy that there is no excuse for not using it.

Next you divide the pack for a riffle shuffle and here you add a little spice to the trick. You riffle the ends of the packets in the usual way but interlace the corners only, and very slightly, Before pushing the cards together furtively break the packets apart and rather hurriedly put the right hand packet on top of the other. You will probably be challenged on this, but whether or no, you repeat the riffle in a way to convince the most sceptical person. Divide the pack by riffling at the back with the right thumb until you reach a red card in the middle and split the deck at that point. The bottom cards of each packet will be reds and the top cards blacks. You have only to riffle shuffle as usual until you see a black card in one hand, hold back the cards in that hand until a black card appears at the bottom of the other packet, then continue dropping cards from each hand alternately to the last card. The pack is once more half red and half black. A surprising result.

THE COPS GET THEIR MAN

EFFECT: From any shuffled deck a card is freely selected. You put the two black Kings openly on the top and bottom of the pack. The selected card is replaced and the pack cut. The Kings are found reversed in the middle. They are taken out, a rubber band is twisted round them and they are pushed through the pack. The chosen card leaves the pack and is found reversed between the shackled Kings.

METHOD: Have a pack shuffled by a spectator and let him retain one card. Take the pack and openly place the King of Clubs on the top and the King of Spades on the bottom. Have the chosen card replaced and bring it to the top by the Side Slip. By means of the Double Lift (C. M. No. 2, p. 22) you show the King of Clubs is still on the top. Leaving this card face up (and the chosen card under it also face up) take the pack by the outer end and turn it over inwards, showing the King of Spades on the bottom. Keep the pack in the same position and draw out the King of Clubs from below, turn it face up and re-place it. The position now is this, on the bottom facing the audience is the King of Spades, on the lower side of the deck is the King of Clubs, facing up and above it the chosen card face downwards.

Grip the ends of the pack between the right thumb at the back, second and third fingers at front end. Let the inner ends of the two lowest cards (K. S. and chosen card) slip off the ball of the thumb and push the rest of deck forward about an inch. Seize the outer end of the deck with right thumb and fingers, the top of the thumb resting on the King of Spades. Push the King of Spades inward about half an inch and turn the rest of the pack over inwards bringing it on top of the King of Spades, which remains face up, under this card is the selected card face down and the King of Clubs face up. See Fig. 11, p. 58, Voraceious Magician, for the method of turning the pack.

You have the spectator cut the cards and you complete the cut. You say you will make the Kings turn over in the deck visibly. You spring the cards from hand to hand and the onlookers get a glimpse of the faces of the two cards as they shoot from hand to hand. Riffle the rear end of the pack till you see the King of Spades, lift off all the cards above it. Under this king will be the chosen card face down, followed by the King of Clubs face up. By the Double Lift (C. M. No. 2 p. 22) take off the King of Spades and the selected card as one, and show the King of Clubs, also face up. Take this up behind the King of Spades, being careful not to expose any part of the card between them. Let the spectator take the pack and shuffle it while you stretch a rubber band around the two Kings lengthways and sideways. You hand this packet to the spectator and let him push it right through the deck, keeping the kings face up.

He then searches the pack for his card, but it has gone. You have it named. The band is taken off the two kings and a card is revealed between them face down. It is the selected card. Presented as a story trick, the King of Clubs being dubbed as Police Sergeant, the rubber band representing handcuffs and so on, you can get a lot of fun and a surprising climax.

Note—For the method of turning the pack see Figs. 10 and 11.

THE PRINCESS TRICK PERFECTED

This trick was originated by Henry Hardin and many variations in its working have been devised. The following routine will be found to extract the greatest effect in the cleanest possible manner using any cards. To begin you take a deck that has been freely shuffled and spreading the cards face up, have four persons each draw a card, the first person to select any Club, the second any Heart, the third any Spade and the fourth any Diamond. You square up the deck in your left hand, keeping it face up, and seize the opportunity to slip the tip of your left little finger under the three lowest cards, that is, the cards next your left palm. Push the rest of the pack forward about one inch, then seize the outer end of the pack and turn it over inwards on top of the three face up cards. See Fig. p. 58.

Spread the cards into a small fan, backs to the front, being careful not to expose any part of the three faced cards. You take the four selected cards and insert them face outwards in fanned pack in same order as they were taken, clubs, hearts, spades, diamonds, allowing about three-quarters of each card to project. Fig. 12. You ask your audience to select a person to act as the transmitter and you ask him to make a mental choice of one of the four cards facing him and then concentrate on that card. In the meantime you have slipped your little finger above the three faced cards at the rear of the fan.

Fig. 12

When the spectator announces that he has fixed on a card, close the fan with your right hand, taking the pack in that hand and removing the four projecting cards with an upward movement of your left hand, which brings up the three reversed cards and thus secretly adds these to the back of the four visible cards. This is a subtle and indetectible sleight. The fact that the backs of the other cards are to the front prevents any idea that any cards can be added to the four removed.

Close the cards in the left hand together tightly, holding the Diamond card facing the front while you place the pack on the table. You turn the seven cards faces towards you and square them exactly with your right hand. Then, take the packet in your right hand, thumb at bottom, fingers at the top, the Diamond facing you and spread the rear cards, the added three to the left with your left hand. Take the cards thus fanned into your left hand. As far as the audience is concerned you have simply spread the four selected cards with their faces towards yourself, in reality these four are held together as one card, the other three are those you secretly added.

Your next move is to take the four cards, as one, and put them in your pocket. First it is necessary to confuse the onlookers as to the relative positions of the cards, so you take out one of the single cards, look at it for a moment, then intently at the transmitter, of course, keeping the back of the card to the front. Shake your head and replace the card in a different place in the fan. Do this several times, finally take the four cards, as one, and place them in your right outside coat pocket. Turn the three cards remaining in the left hand face downward and deal them on to the deck, counting "One, Two, Three". Casually cut the pack and complete the cut, getting the three out of the way. You have now to get the name of the card selected; do not bluntly ask for it but address the transmitter to this effect: "Now if I have succeeded in reading your thoughts, or rather, if you have transmitted the correct mental impression to me, then I have your card in my pocket. You know, and I know, that we have not made any prior arrangement about the experiment, but to satisfy everyone that you are not helping me in any way whatever, will you, please, name the card you have in mind? The Six of Clubs? I knew it. The impression you sent was so strong there could be no mistake. Here it is. The Six of Clubs."

It will have been noted that the four cards are taken in the familiar Charlier order, Clubs, Hearts, Spades, Diamonds. The key-word for this is CHaSeD, so that the moment the card is named you know which of the four to bring out and you do it with no hesitation whatever. Properly presented before suitable audiences the feat may well be accepted as a genuine telepathic experiment.

THE THREE CARD TRICK AS A TRICK AND

NOT A GAMBLE

This gambler's trick depends upon a subtle change. The sleight is easily acquired with just a little practice. I know of no other card feat which will repay the student as fully as this. It can be made to provide endless amusement, and unlike other card feats, repetition enhances the effect. Before describing a routine in which the sleight is used to create a series of mystifying changes, in place of the usual gambling game, a brief explanation of the correct method of executing the sleight is necessary.

THE THROW

Place two cards together and bend them lengthwise, making the faces concave, so that they may be easily picked up by the ends. Lay them on the table separately, face down. Take one by the ends, near the right side corners, between the right thumb and second finger. Place this card over the other so that their left sides touch and pick up the lower card between the thumb and third finger, with a space of about half an inch between the right hand sides of the two cards, the forefinger rests on the top of the upper card.

To make the change you apparently throw the lower card face down on the table and drop the other alongside it. In reality the top card is thrown first. To do this you move your hand with a slight swing towards the left, release the top card and quickly draw the hand back to its former position. At the same moment drop the tip of the second finger on the corner of the lower card and straighten out the third finger. The onlooker sees the second finger still holding the upper card, as he thinks, and when this is put down he has no suspicion that the cards have changed places.

If you take the positions EXACTLY as described you will have no difficulty in acquiring the sleight. In practise you should really throw the lower card first, then execute the change, imitating the moves just made.

THREE CARD ROUTINE

The best cards to use are the seven and eight of hearts and the ace of spades. Lay these cards, after bending them, face down in a row. Red. Black. Red.

Position   R2   B   R1

Lift the cards one by one, show their faces and replace them. Take up R1, show its face, with it cover R2, turn and show face, throw R2 down without change, turn R1, show face, and with it cover B which you turn and show. Throw B (no change) on table a little forward toward spectator, finally turn R1, show face and throw down on right side.

B

Position   R2   R1

Again lift R1 and show, cover R2, show and throw R2, (no change). Show R1, cover B and show. You ask spectator to place his hand on the Black card and you throw it down towards him. This time you make the change and throw R1, on which he puts his hand. At once cover R2 with B, and show. Throw B (change) to right, turn hand and show R2, which you drop to the left.

R1

Position   B   R2

You pass your hand over your two cards, then over spectator's hand and back over your cards, saying that you are taking the red off your cards and passing it to his, and the black from his cards to yours. He lifts his card, it is Red. You lift R2, not showing its face, cover B and turn and show, throw R2 (change). Again turn B and show face, then drop it to the right.

                                              R1
                          Position   R2   B

Now you show your two cards Red by taking B and with it as cover lifting R2 which you turn and show, throw B (change) turn and show R2 again.

                                              R1
                          Position   B   R2

Show all three Red by lifting B, with it cover R1, throw B (change). Cover R2 with R1, turn and show. Throw R2 (no change) to left of B, turn R1, show and throw to right of B. **Position R2 B R1**

Pass your hand over B, lift and show B has returned. Put down in the middle again. Lift R1, cover B and show, throw R1 (change), with B cover R2, lift and show R2, throw B (change) to right, show R2 and throw to left.   **Position   R2   R1   B**

Fig. 13

Make a motion of passing B from middle to right. Lift B, show and replace at right. **Position   R2   R1   B**

Next show all as Red. With B as cover, pick up R1, show and throw B (change). With R1 as cover pick up R2 and show. Throw R2 to left of B (no change), show R1 and throw to right.   **Position   R2   B   R1**

Now show all as Black. Pick up R1, cover B, turn and show B. Throw R1 (change) to right. Drop B. Pick up R2, cover B, lift and show B. Throw R2 (change). Drop B then lift and show it. All have been shown Black.

Finally gather up all three one on the other and throw them down faces up. You have two Red and one Black as at the start.

It is essential to success that when you hold two cards in the hand to make the throw or show the lower card the outside edges must not touch and coincide. Fig. 13. If you wish to make a reputation for phenomenal dexterity with cards with the least possible time required for practise, then master this routine. It is based on one by M. Nordach in Gaultier's book, "Prestidigitation sans Appariels."

For further details and moves relating to Three Card Monte see the exhaustive treatise by Scarne and Walsh.

THE PUSH-OUT FALSE CUT

Many card players who have an inkling of the possibilities of false shuffling make a point when cutting, of pushing a packet out from the middle and placing it on the top or bottom. Fairly done this would upset any arrangement of the cards. It is convincing for the magician to appear to do this when cutting a set-up deck.

You hold the pack in the left hand between the first joints of the second and third fingers on one side and the thumb on the other, right side of the body to the front. With the tip of the right forefinger push out a dozen or more cards, making them project about an inch from the front end of the deck.

Take this packet by the sides between the right thumb and second finger and draw it out at the same moment let all the cards below drop on the left palm as in the Charlier pass.

Under cover of the right wrist and forearm complete the pass by pushing this packet up against the left thumb with the forefinger and allowing the top packet to fall on it. Bring the right hand back over these cards and drop its packet on them.

The action leaves the pack as it would be if one complete cut had been made. The sleight is new, easy and convincing.

FALSE CUT FOR SET-UP DECK

Hold pack in left hand and regard it as being divided into three packets A, B and C.

With right hand take off about one-third, packet A, and drop this on the table.

Take the rest of deck in right hand and drop about half of these cards from below, Packet C, on top of A, letting them project slightly at the front edge. Drop the last packet, B, in front of these two packets.

Pick up C A with right hand, fingers at outer end, thumb at inner end, pressing down slightly on the overlapping edge of C, making a break which is held by the thumb as the packets are slid back to edge of table to raise them.

Drop lower packet A on top of B and throw C down in front of A B. Take up A B and drop on C. The pack is again in its original order. The cuts should be made quickly and the action will convince anyone that the cards have been mixed.

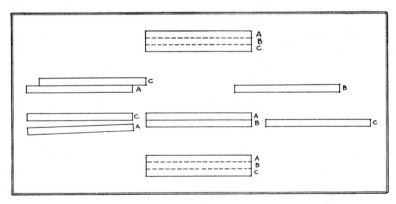

Fig. 14

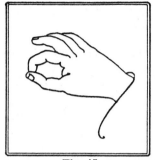

Fig. 15

Fig. 16

Fig. 17

Fig. 18

AN AERIAL PRODUCTION

For this startling production of a fan of cards from the air, you palm about a dozen cards faces inward, in your right hand. The rest of the pack is in your left hand and you stand with your left side to the front.

Holding your right hand high with its back to the onlookers, you make a catch in the air, bringing the thumb and forefinger together as in Fig. 15. This illustration is not exactly correct. The first and second fingers hold the cards therefore you can not elevate the second finger—it is the third and fourth fingers which are raised and spread apart.

Fig. 16 is a rear view of the hand and shows how the cards are concealed.

Separate thumb and finger, keeping the other fingers in the same relative positions, and make a second catch but, this time, close the fingers on the back of the palmed packet and grip the cards near their inner ends between the thumb and fingers, Fig. 17. Instantly spread the cards fanwise, thumb moving to the right and fingers to the left, Fig. 18.

The sleight is a very easy one to learn. A few minutes practise before a mirror to get the correct angle at which to hold the hand is all that is necessary. It will be found that the cards come automatically into the right position for fanning them.

This production is really more surprising than that from the back of the hand. The position in which the hand is held seems to preclude any possibility of concealment and the instantaneous appearance of a large fan of cards is astonishing, even to a magician, if he is not familiar with the sleight.

THE FLOURISH COUNT

In such tricks as "The Cards to the Pocket", you have occasion to count off ten or twelve cards, and it is necessary to do it in such a way that it is obvious to every one that you are taking off one card at a time.

You hold the pack face down in your left hand. With the thumb push off the top card about an inch, bend the tip of the forefinger under it and press the tip of the second finger on its back. The top card is thus gripped between the first joints of the first two fingers. Straighten them out, carrying the card outwards and turning it face up in transit. Fig. 19. The third and little fingers are lifted slightly to let the card pass and are then closed on the deck again. The deck should be pressed well into the fork of the thumb.

Fig. 19

Take the card in your right hand, counting "One", and repeat the movement with as many cards as may be required for the trick you are doing.

WEAVING THE CARDS

THE EFFECT: The pack is squared and then divided as for the riffle shuffle. A packet is held in each hand, by the ends, the free ends are placed together and the cards are interweaved, card for card, in very pretty fashion.

THE METHOD: The pack must be squared perfectly and in good condition. A new pack will give best results. You take the deck with both hands, holding it by the ends, thumb on one side, second and third fingers on the other, the first fingers resting on top of the packets. Divide the pack as nearly as possible in halves and draw the packets apart. Fig. I. Keeping each half squared, place their inner corners together.

Push the packets inward so that their free ends bend upwards. It will be found that the ends of the packets will become wedge-shaped as they are bent up one against the other, and the cards will naturally tend to fall alternately from each packet. In fact the action becomes a kind of riffle shuffle.

There is a knack in the sleight that can only be acquired by practice. The effect is so pretty that it is well worth while to devote the time to it necessary to master it. The Weave is most useful in the making of the Giant Fan and the Double Arm Spread.

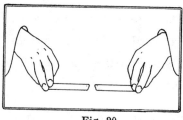 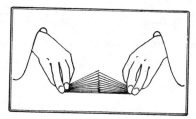

Fig. 20   Fig. 21

THE GIANT FAN

I. THE FORMATION

You hold the pack face down, divide it into two portions, as nearly equal as possible, and riffle shuffle them together, dropping the cards from each hand alternately. The first and last cards should be dropped from the left hand. If you have acquired the Weave, p. 72, use it instead of riffle.

The two packets, thus interlaced, are held in the left hand as in Fig. 22, the left thumb being just below the top of the face card of the lower packet and the left fingers in the same position at the back. The cards of the two packets should be exactly in line giving the deck the appearance of having been pulled out to nearly twice its length. It will now be seen why the first and last cards were dropped from the left hand first and last. It is by pressure on these two cards that the protruding cards are held in place.

Bring your right hand over and place the thumb across the face of the packets at the point of junction, just at the top of the face card of the lower packet, the ball of the thumb resting on the left side of the elongated pack and the fingers extended behind. With the left thumb press firmly against the fingers, keeping the cards of the upper packet in place, while your right thumb, slipping over the sides of the pack as the hand moves to the right in a circular sweep, spreads the cards into a large fan. Fig. 23. At the end of the movement the four cards at the bottom of the fan should be in a straight line across the hand. Fig. 24.

Fig. 22

Fig. 23

NOTE:—Fig. 23 is not exactly correct. Thumb should be lower across the face of the packets at the point of junction, just at the top of the face card of the lower packet.

Fig. 24

II. FANNING YOURSELF

You exhibit the fan, holding the left hand high, the faces of the cards to the front, and wave the cards, gently fanning yourself, just as you would do with a real fan. A firm downward pressure of the thumb will keep the protruding cards in position.

III. CLOSING AND OPENING THE FAN

Place your right thumb in front of the outer side of the fan, the fingers at the back, then with a quick upward movement of the right hand close the fan sharply. At once spread it again to its fullest extent. If you maintain the firm pressure of the left thumb throughout you will have no difficulty in keeping the cards in perfect order. This move has a very pretty effect.

IV. CLOSING THE FAN WITH ONE HAND

You open and close the fan two or three times, then with it open you extend your left arm about shoulder high and close the fan with the left hand only. To do this you hold your left hand palm upwards, the cards at the right hand side of the fan resting at the base of the little finger, with the tips of the first and second fingers at the back of the fan push the cards over and downwards toward the right, still maintaining the firm pressure of the ball of the left thumb. At the end of the action the packets should lie vertically on their sides on the left palm.

V. FINISH OF THE GIANT FAN MOVES

With the elongated pack lying as described on its side upright extend the fingers and let the cards fall face up. With the right thumb and fingers seize the two packets at the point of junction and hold them firmly, then with left hand take hold of the end of the left packet and with the right hand seize the packet on the right. You now have one end of the elongatad deck in each hand. Hold the cards lightly so that the ends do not bind and draw the packets apart, immediately fanning each portion. Run the faces of the cards two or three times, one packet against the other, with an up and down movement of the hands, put them one on the other and square the deck.

There is really no difficult move in the routine, yet the effect produced is not only pleasing but gives the onlookers a high opinion of the performer's skill.

VANISH OF DECK

EFFECT:

A deck of cards is wrapped in a handkerchief and both are tossed into the air, the cards vanish.

PREPARATION:

To the middle of a handkerchief sew an oblong shape of thin wire exactly the size of the end of a deck. The wire should be enameled white.

The handkerchief, so folded that when it is spread out the shape will be on the side away from the audience, is placed in your right coat pocket on the outside.

METHOD:

After a series of tricks with cards you place the whole pack in your left hand apparently, really you palm off about half the cards in your right hand. You hold the cards in the left hand squarely towards the front so that the diminished number is not noticeable. With your right hand take the handkerchief from your pocket, leaving the palmed cards behind.

Spread the handkerchief with the shape on the side towards you by taking a corner in each hand. Place your left hand with the remaining half of the deck at the middle of the handkerchief at the back and let the handkerchief fall over the hand. Seize the wire shape with the right hand from above and palm the cards in your left hand. At once bring this hand from under the handkerchief, back of the hand to the front, and make a pretense of draping the fabric around the deck.

Standing with your right side to the front you suddenly toss the handkerchief into the air and as it falls, catch it by a corner and shake it vigorously. At the same moment you drop the palmed cards from your left hand into your outside left coat pocket. The lappel of this pocket should have been pushed in previously. The cards have vanished in thin air.

When wrapping the pack do not say anything about vanishing the cards. You talk about the pack being a valuable one and you always take great care of it. The actual vanish should come as a complete surprise.

SERIES 4

Card Manipulations No. 4

CONTENTS

SECTION 1—SLEIGHTS

1. TO PALM A NUMBER OF CARDS FROM THE TOP

Palming is probably the weakest spot in the technique of most card workers, both amateur and professional. The most common faults being the manner in which the hand is brought right over the deck, taking off the required cards with a perceptible grabbing acfion, at the same time telegraphing the movement by throwing the thumb straight upward and, finally, the removal of the hand with the cards in it without any reason at all having been given for the whole action. Under these circumstances it would have to be a very innocent spectator who did not suspect that some cards had been removed from the pack.

To palm cards perfectly the action must be so covered that a spectator who keeps his eyes fixed on the performer's hands can detect no suspicious movement. This is not so difficult as might be imagined and the method that follows is well within the reach of any card handler with a minimum of practice.

I do not know who originated the move but it has been in use amongst some experts for years and the general belief is that we are indebted for it to the same source from which have come many of the most subtle card sleights—the gambling table. Hence I have dubbed the. move—

THE GAMBLER'S TOP PALM

To execute the sleight proceed as follows:

1. Hold the pack in the left hand by its sides between the first joints of the thumb and the second and third fingers, the first joint of the forefinger being doubled under the pack and resting against the bottom card, the tip of the little finger being inserted in the pack under the cards to be palmed. Fig. 1.

2. Bring the right hand over the deck, the fingers held closely together, covering the outer end, and the ball of the thumb touching the inner end, the hand being arched naturally over the deck.

3. Move the right hand towards the right and back again in the usual motion of squaring the ends of the cards with the tips of the fingers and the thumb.

4. Grip the pack between the right thumb and fingers, releasing it from the hold of the left fingers and thumb, and move them outwards as if merely squaring the sides of the deck, but in this action the first joint of the left little finger levers the cards above it upwards into the right palm, being assisted in the movement by the tip of the left thumb on the opposite side of the deck. Fig. 2.

5. The right hand must be held motionless as the cards are pushed up and palmed. The pack is again gripped by the left hand as in move No. 1, and the right fingers and thumb are slid along the ends of the deck, squaring them as before.

6. Finally seize the pack with the right hand at the outer top and bottom corners, at the same time extend the left middle finger and with it push against the middle of the palmed packet, pressing it securely into the palm.

7. Remove the left hand leaving the pack gripped by the right hand at the outer top and bottom corners between the forefinger and thumb and bend the other three fingers inwards a little, bending the cards in towards the palm. Fig. 3.

Note particularly that speed is not required, the action should be simply the apparent squaring of the ends and sides of the deck. Reference to the One Hand Top Palm on p. 2, C. M. 1, will show that the principle is the same but, in place of one card only, any required number of cards can be palmed indetectibly.

THE CHANGE-OVER PALM

This very useful sleight appears to be known to but few present-day card manipulators although it is a very old move. The reason for this may be that it has never been explained in any of the textbooks on card sleights. By its means a card or packet of cards can be transferred imperceptibly from one hand to the other, the effect to the onlooker being that both hands are empty. The procedure is as follows:

A. WITH SMALL PACKET OF CARDS ONLY

1. Standing with left side to the front, a packet of cards being palmed in the left hand, hold the right hand palm towards the audience, the arm bent and the fingers pointing upwards. Bring the left hand over to the right, extend the left forefinger and with it lightly touch the empty right palm, the cards being held securely by bending the other three fingers inward slightly. Fig. 4.

2. Make a half turn to the left, under cover of which, as the right hand moves in front to the left, bend the left forefinger inward and with it grip the outer index corner of the cards, pressing them firmly against the base of the thumb. Release the other three fingers of the left hand and bend them in behind the cards, thus bending the packet outwards. Fig. 5.

3. At the moment that you face the audience squarely and the back of the right hand is towards the front, straighten out the left second, third and fourth fingers and spring the cards into the right hand. Fig. 6.

4. Complete the turn to the left bringing the now empty left palm to the front, extend the right forefinger, bend the other three fingers in towards the palm and with the forefinger touch the left palm. Fig. 7.

The sleight is not at all difficult but must be done smoothly. The actual transfer of the cards from one hand to the other is imperceptible if made at the right moment. The action should be practiced before a mirror.

Two faults must be guarded against; one is the tendency to let the thumbs fly straight upwards as the cards are palmed. They should lie flat in an easy natural position throughout. The other is, allowing the cards to make a distinct click as they are sprung from one hand to the other. The transfer must be noiseless as well as invisible.

B. WITH THE PACK IN HAND

Hold the pack in the left hand and palm the packet to be transferred by means of the bottom palm in the left hand. (Erdnase, p. 86.) Immediately afterwards carry the pack away towards the right with the right hand, holding it between the thumb and fingers by the outer top and bottom corners, and making a gesture appropriate to the patter used, to show the right hand empty.

2. Replace the pack flat in the fork of the left thumb. At the moment that the back of the right hand is towards the front, bend the left second, third and fourth fingers in behind the palmed packet and spring the cards into the right hand as in the first method A.

There must be no noise and the thumbs must lie naturally against the sides of the hands. The action takes place under cover of a swing from right to left and when the transfer has been made the left hand should be so held that all can see it holds the pack only.

A NEW TOP CHANGE

This sleight will be found to be an easy and indetectible method of transposing the first and second cards of the pack. The moves are as follows:

1. Turn the top card face up by pushing it over the side of the pack with the left thumb and then bringing the right from below it so that the upper side of the right forefinger strikes against the card at its outer edge. Fig. 8.

2. With the left thumb push this faced card and the next card below it outwards over the side of the deck and put the right hand flat on the faced card, covering about one half of it, the outer half. Fig. 9.

3. With the left thumb pull the faced card back over the pack and, at the same time, with the tips of the left fingers, push the card below it into the right palm. The right hand must be held stationary.

4. Turn the faced card over, bringing it face down on the pack, with the side of the right forefinger by bringing that hand upwards in exactly the same way as in move No. 1, the tips of the second and third fingers assist in lifting the outer edge of the card.

5. Deposit the palmed card on top and draw the right hand fingers and thumb along the top and bottom ends of the pack in the action of squaring the cards.

This sleight will be found specially useful in working "The Ambitious Card Trick" wherein a card repeatedly placed in the middle of the pack always appears on the top. It should be executed in exact imitation of the manner in which the card is first turned by move No. 1. Smoothly done the change is imperceptible.

REPLACING PALMED CARDS

Apart from a casual reference by Erdnase, I do not recall mention of this important sleight in any of the text books on card magic. That it is important and a stumbling block to many card magicians is quite certain. Recently, I saw a performer, who has a great reputation for his work with cards, do a trick of the "Take a Card Variety". Having allowed a spectator to choose a card and replace it, he made the pass very clumsily, palmed the card in his right hand which he at once put behind his back as he offered the pack with his left hand to the drawer of the card to be shuffled. To take the pack back again he extended his left hand to receive it and then deliberately put his right hand on the deck replacing the card on top. This clumsy procedure made his trick quite obvious even to the uninitiated.

The following methods will show how the awkardness of taking the pack back with the left hand can be avoided and the whole action covered by natural movements:

1. USING A TABLE

When working at or near a table, after bringing the chosen card to the top, palm it by means of the One Hand Top Palm (Card Manipulations, No. 1, p. 2) in handing the deck to be shuffled. When this has been done ask the spectator to place the deck on the table and cut it. As he lifts off the upper portion of the pack place your right hand on the remaining packet and draw it back towards the edge of the table in the natural way of picking the deck up, adding the palmed card (or cards) to the top and covering operation with the full width of the hand.

Take the cut portion from the spectator with your left hand, place the right hand packet on top of it and square the deck. These actions are natural and can arouse no suspicions.

The tendency to hold the hand and arm rigidly to the side when cards have been palmed, must be fought against. The wrist and arm should be held naturally flexed and be moved about freely in gestures appropriate to your patter, indeed the fact that cards are secretly held in the hand should be forgotten for the moment.

2. WITHOUT A TABLE

When working without a table the best plan is this: A card, or cards, having been palmed in the right hand and a spectator having shuffled a pack, hold out your left hand, flat and palm upwards, request him to place the deck on it and then cut at any place he desires. The moment he lifts the cut portion bring your right hand over the remainder adding the palmed cards to them and at once bend the right forefinger inward to the middle of the top of the packet. Press downwards with this finger and pull the ends of the cards upwards with the thumb and fingers on the ends, thus taking the crimp out of the cards that were palmed. Take the cut portion from the spectator with the left hand and reassemble the pack.

Here again the action is easy and natural, and so far from arousing any suspicion in the minds of the spectators, it tends to impress them that the cut so freely made must make it certain that the location of any particular card cannot possibly be known.

3. REPLACING CARDS ON THE BOTTOM OF THE DECK

The operation in this case is simple but must be timed perfectly. Having palmed a packet of cards from the bottom with the left hand, offer the deck to be shuffled with your right hand, and this having been done, take it back with the same hand. Bring the two hands together, the left coming up from the side with its back to the spectators. At the moment the hands meet turn the left hand palm upwards and with the right hand place the deck, which holds by the ends, on the palmed cards. At the same time double the left forefinger under the deck so that its nail rests against the bottom card, and run the left thumb and the other three fingers along the sides of the deck squaring the cards. Fig. 10.

A few trials before a mirror will show the angles necessary to cover the replacement of the palmed cards.

4. ADDING A SINGLE CARD AS IN THE COLOR CHANGE

This sleight is generally done with the pack in the left hand, the left thumb being held against the side of the deck. It is much more effective to hold the thumb pressed against the middle of the deck, so that when the right hand is moved over the cards, the left thumb is seen to be still pressing on the middle of the face card, yet the change has been made. To do this, hold the pack in the left hand, the thumb across the middle of the face card.

Bring the right hand with the palmed card towards the deck, at the same time press the first joint of the right hand little finger against the corner of the palmed card and push its opposite diagonal corner firmly against the base of the thumb, thus bending the middle of the card slightly away from the palm of the hand. Fig. 11

Move the right hand over the deck and, without moving the left thumb, slide the card under it and leave it there. As the right hand moves away the left thumb is seen to be still pressing on the middle of the deck, thus greatly increasing the effect of the change.

The same method should be used for placing a card, secured by the Side Slip, on to the top of the pack, the action apparently being that of merely squaring the deck. The left thumb should remain on the back of the deck throughout.

This sleight can be used in replacing a small packet of not more than five or six cards. For any larger number the plan that follows should be used.

5. TO REPLACE A LARGE PACKET OF CARDS

Hold the pack in the left hand between the first joints of the thumb and second and third fingers, the first finger being doubled under the deck so that its nail presses against the bottom card.

Turn slightly to the left, bring the right hand full length over the deck and instantly grip its ends with the ball of the thumb at the inner end and the first joints of the second and third fingers at the outer end, depositing the palmed cards on top of the deck. Instantly bend the right forefinger inwards so that its tip rests on the middle of the top card. Press down with forefinger and pull the ends of the deck slightly upwards, so taking the bend out of the cards which were palmed. Fig. 12.

6. ANOTHER METHOD

Having cards palmed in the right hand, hold the deck as described in move No. 5. Turn slightly to the left and take the pack with the right hand by gripping its outer top and bottom corners between the first joints of the right forefinger and thumb. The backs of the right hand and the deck should be towards the front. Making some appropriate gesture with the left hand allow it to be seen empty and and again take the pack in that hand. At the same moment slide the right hand over the top of the deck and grip the palmed pack by

its sides with the left thumb and fingers. Slide the right hand back
as if it had merely squared the cards.

7. PLACING CARDS FROM RIGHT PALM TO THE BOTTOM OF THE DECK

Proceed as in Move No. 6, but instead of sliding the right hand
over the deck, stretch out the left fingers under the deck and, under
cover of the right hand, draw the palmed cards underneath. To
facilitate this transfer, lift the right hand side of the deck slightly
with the right thumb and first finger. The moment the cards are
safely under the deck make the usual movements with the right
hand to square the cards.

8. ANOTHER METHOD

This sleight can only be used when working at a table. A packet
of cards being palmed in the right hand, to get them to the bottom,
take the deck in both hands by the ends and make a running cut, i. e.
draw off a series of small packets from the top and drop them on
the table. The apparent removal of the first packet is merely a feint;
simply make the action but take no cards at all, dropping the palmed
cards on the table. Then really make the cuts with precisely the
same action as in the first pretended cut. The palmed cards thus
become the bottom cards of the deck.

SOME NOTES ON THE PASS

In spite of all the printer's ink which has been spilled in describing this sleight it still remains a stumbling block in the path of the
tyro. In order to avoid its use much ingenuity has been exercised
to find satisfactory substitutes for it. Some of these are useful, so
useful indeed, that some of our best card men have told me that
only on rare occasions do they have recourse to the pass. However,
the fact that they do have to use it sometimes shows that it is necessary for the would-be card manipulator to master it. The difficulty
found in its execution arises mainly from an imperfect understanding of the moves required.

So many descriptions of the sleight have appeared that it will
not be necessary to enter into all the details here. The main point
to be noted is this—the upper half of the deck must be gripped firmly
between the top joints of the first three fingers of the left hand, above,
and the first joint of the little finger below. The lower portion of the
pack must be held between the tips of the right thumb and second
finger, the right hand being arched as much as possible above the
pack, which is held at an angle of about forty-five degrees. By
straightening the lowest joints of the left fingers with the back of the
hand, the top portion is **drawn** off to the right, it is not **lifted** off. The
right second finger then lifts the lower portion slightly by bending its
first joint inwards, the hand itself remaining motionless. The arch
of the right hand affords room for the edges of the packets to clear
one another, the left fingers are then closed, the two packets having
changed places.

It requires rare skill to make the pass invisibly with the hands at rest, but that this can be done, those who have seen Mr. Ralph W. Read perform the sleight will testify. But it is not necessary to attain such extraordinary dexterity. A recent visitor to the U. S. A., Mr. John Ramsey, an accomplished magician from Ayr, Scotland, showed that, after the position of the hands for the pass has been taken, if they are then raised slightly and turned over to show the fact of the bottom card, the pass can be made imperceptibly in turning the hands back with a downward motion. It is interesting to note that a French writer, M. Ponsin, early in the last century, described the same moves as being a perfect cover for the execution of the pass.

I have found that it aids greatly in disguising the sleight, if at the very moment that the pass is completed, the hands are moved a little apart, spreading the cards, with the accompaniment of some such remark as this: "You see the card remains in the middle of the deck." Then close the pack sharply and go into an overhand shuffle without an instant's delay .

If the movements described above are done smoothly and boldly, while addressing the drawer of the card and looking him in the face, the actual transposition need not be very rapid, yet the operation will be completely covered. It is misdirection, not the rapidity, that counts.

SUBSTITUTES FOR THE PASS

A great number of different moves have been evolved for controlling a chosen card without the use of the pass. By request I give three of the best.

No. 1 — THE BREAK AND OVERHAND SHUFFLE

A card having been drawn do not simply cut the pack for its replacement, a suspicious and inartistic procedure. Rather spread the pack fanwise and as the person extends his hand with the card, divide the fan about the middle, push it forward and actually take the card from him, for all the world as if you were using a forceps. You do not, of course, snatch the card, but work smoothly and without hesitation. Instantly close the fan, inserting the tip of the left little finger above the card.

Remove your right hand for a moment, allowing all to see that the outer end of the pack is closed and regular. Fig. 13.

Take the pack, from above between t h e right second finger, at the outer end, and the ball of the right thumb, at the inner end. Press the t h u m b tightly against the pack, retaining the break made by the left little finger. Remove your left hand for a moment making some gesture, appropriate to your patter, again allowing the outer end of the pack to be visible, the break at the back being out of sight, unless you allow someone to stand directly behind you. Fig. 14.

Proceed to an overhand shuffle by placing the pack in the fork of your left thumb, which then turns the pack down as if it were pivoted at the tips of the right second finger and thumb of your right hand, the break being retained by the ball of the thumb. Fig. 15.

Shuffle the cards in the usual way until the break is reached, then throw the rest of the cards on top. The chosen card is thus brought to the top of the pack, ready to be dealt with in any way desired for the purpose of the trick in hand, without any irregular or quick movement; indeed, the sleight should be executed rather slowly, giving the onlooker every opportunity of seeing how honest the procedure appears from the front.

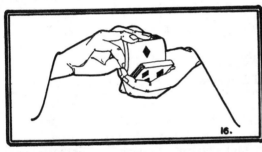

No. 2
The Riffle Return

In this method you allow the drawer of the card to push it into the deck as you riffle the outer end. Prevent the card from going flush with the rest by holding the inner end of the pack tightly. Fig. 16.

Draw the deck back, covering it with the right hand, and, under cover of squaring the cards, push the outer end of the card a little over to the left and then downward diagonally, so that its left top and right bottom corners protrude slightly from the deck. The left little finger at once straightens the card by pressing on the right lower corner. The selected card will now project from the lower end of the pack. Fig. 17, A, B and C.

Divide the deck at the projecting card, taking off the top half, and this card, with the right hand, and proceed at once to a riffle shuffle. The position in which the cards are held allows you to sight the chosen card without arousing any suspicion on the part of the spectators. You may put it at the bottom of the pack by allowing it to drop first, or you may place it second, third or fourth from the bottom by letting one, two or three cards drop from the left hand packet first.

Illustrations Nos. A, B and C are exaggerated for the sake of clearness. The card should protrude an eigth of an inch at the utmost, and, with practise, it may be allowed to project so slightly as to be practically imperceptible except to the touch.

No. 3. REVERSED CARDS AS INDICATOR

This is rather a barefaced procedure, but it is very useful at times to baffle a sceptical spectator who may have an inkling of the usual methods. In spreading the cards for one to be chosen push the bottom card well into the fork of the left thumb, then, as you close the pack, lift all except this card slightly. At the same moment, press the tips of the right fingers against the right side of this bottom card and move the left hand to the right, so that the card is turned face up under the rest of the cards. The move is made under cover of closing the spread of card and is imperceptible.

While the card is being noted, make a free overhand shuffle, simply retaining the bottom card in position. Then undercut about half the deck, have the card replaced on the portion in the left hand and drop the undercut on top. Square the deck very openly and tap both sides and ends on the table, plainly showing that there is no break or jogged card, but be careful not to mention these artifices. If any of your audience know about these processes they can see you are using them, so why suggest them to others who are ignorant of their possible use. You may have occasion to use them in another trick later on.

To get control of the chosen card and right the reversed card, you may divide the deck, riffling the inner end with the right thumb, dividing the pack at the reversed card, and, by a riffle shuffle, send that card to the bottom and the chosen card to the top. Pull up your left sleeve with the right hand and with the pack in the left hand pull up your right sleeve. It is an easy matter then to turn the bottom card over with the fingers against the sleeve under cover of the forearm.

Or, standing with your right side to the front, shuffle the pack overhand. Shuffle freely till you have almost reached the reversed card, then run the cards off singly When the reversed card shows up, thumb it right off the pack and let it fall on the floor. At once drop the rest of the cards on top of those shuffled off into your left hand, thus bringing the drawn card to the top. Apologize for your clumsiness and pick up the fallen card, casually inquiring if it is the selected cards, as if you didn't know.

The use of these three entirely different means of controlling a card, combined with an occasional regular pass, will throw the onlookers entirely off the trail. It is advisable, when working out the details of a particular trick to apply one of these methods to it and thereafter stick to that particular move for that trick. This will help in attaining that smoothness of execution which is so necessary to success.

TWO USEFUL MOVES

I have mentioned in my other books the reversing of a card against the thigh and I have been asked to give a detailed description of the move. This little slight is very useful and by it, too, a card can be transferred imperceptibly from the top to the bottom of the deck.

1. TO REVERSE THE BOTTOM CARD

Hold the deck in the left hand which you drop casually to your side as you make a gesture with the right hand, appropriate to the patter used.

With the left thumb resting against the thigh, push the bottom card down until its upper edge is gripped by the tips of the thumb and fingers, Fig. 18; then slide the fingers out over the back of the card and close them, thus turning the card over against the bottom of the pack. Fig. 19.

Make a very slight turn to the left as the sleight is executed, taking the left hand and the pack out of sight for a moment only. Then bring the left hand up with its back to the front. By holding the pack, face upwards, the top card can be reversed in the same way.

2. TO TRANSFER THE BOTTOM CARD TO THE TOP

Proceed in exactly the same way to begin with, but push the bottom card right off the pack, then press the tips of your fingers on its lower side and slide the pack under it, the fingers drawing the card up on to the top.

3. A GAMBLER'S MOVE

The sleight described above is akin to a gambler's move which is useful to the magician on occasion. In this case it is made under cover of the right forearm. Let us suppose that the pack has been cut and you hold a break between the two packets with the tip of your little finger. You wish to make a pass, change the packets to their original positions. You are smoking, sitting at table.

Take your cigar, or cigarette, and put it to your left on the edge of the table. As you bring your right arm across, passing it in front of the left hand and the cards, you rest the upper side of the pack against your sleeve, draw out the lower portion from under the break by extending the left fingers, and as the sides of the packets clear one another, push the lower packet forward and draw the other packet back under it with your fingers.

The move can be made in a moment and is completely under cover. It is used by the gambler to reverse the cut just before he begins the deal. As he puts down his cigar, he makes some remark about the stakes for instance, reverses the cut and he is all set to trim his opponents as usual.

CARD TRICKS

A NOVEL REVERSE DISCOVERY

The following trick, for which I am indebted to that master card artiste, Mr. Nate Leipzig, is a fine addition to the most desirable class of card feats, those that can be done at any time with any deck of cards.

The pack having been shuffled by a spectator you allow him free choice of a card by having him simply lift the outer corner of the deck at any point and note the index of a card. Holding the break side, slip the card to the top and thoroughly shuffle the pack, finishing by running the card to the bottom.

Then ask the spectator to hold out his left hand flat and palm upwards and, as he does this, palm the card from the bottom in the left hand. Holding this hand as flat as possible, place it over his left hand, palm downwards, of course, and about half an inch away. Place the deck face down lengthways on the back of your left hand.

The spectator then names his card and you pat the back of the deck with your right hand, at the same moment relaxing your grip of the palmed card which falls face up on the spectator's hand, being so revealed as you remove your left hand and the pack.

The effect of the chosen card apparently pasing through the deck and your hand, turning face up in so doing, is quite startling to the uninitiated.

The Erdnase Diagonal Shift Palm could be used effectively in this trick. In this case the card would be drawn from the pack by the spectator, replaced by him and palmed in the left hand in the act of handing the pack to him to be shuffled.

THE RISING PACK

This trick makes a very good opener for a series of feats with cards. It is quick, mysterious and indetectable. The effect is that the whole pack rises spontaneously from its case, both case and cards being immediately handed for examination.

The preparation is simple, depending on the magician's good friend, a length of fine black silk. To one end tie a safety pin, the

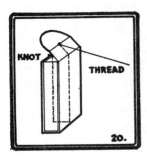

other end you pass through a tiny hole in the back of a card case, from the back towards the front. In the middle of the front edge of the case cut out a small slit and, making a knot at the end of the thread, engage it in the slit. The silk thus runs across the mouth of the case and if the pack is dropped in it will carry the thread down with it. Fig. 20. A pull on the silk from the back causes the pack to rise.

To work the trick, fasten the safety pin (black) inside your upper left vest pocket, attaching it to the inside lining, fix the thread as described above and drop the pack in the case; push the flap in the case and put it in the vest pocket, aranging the slack of the thread carefully behind the case so that it will pull out straight.

You propose to show some feats with cards and you feel several pockets for your pack, as if you didn't remember in which one you had put it, finally, bring it out of the vest pocket and put it in the left hand. With the right hand pull the flap up, hold it with the front of the case towards the audience, and make a motion of taking the pack out. Pause and say, "But I am forgetting. My cards are well trained. I don't even have to take them out of the case myself—watch." Push only the tip of the flap in again and extend the left hand till the silk is taut. "Cards, Rise," you command. Stretch your left hand very slowly straight out away from you, holding the case firmly and waving your right hand over it. The cards will rise and forcing the flap back, will gradually come into view. Do not raise the left hand for an upward motion would be perceptible, a straight outward and slow movement will not be noticed, all attention being on the cards as they rise out of the case.

When the pack is almost completely out, take the cards in your right hand by their upper ends and raise the hand high with a triumphant gesture, "You see how obedient they are," you say. At the same moment drop the left hand with the case to your side rather sharply. This action will pull the silk out of the little slit and through the hole in the case and you can at once hand both cards and case to a spectator to be examined. The silk will fall under the left side of the coat and will be quite out of the way.

It will be found that this little feat will arouse the interested attention of any audience and put them in the proper frame of mind for the reception of other marvels.

HOW TO MAKE A SPECTATOR BECOME A MAGICIAN

This is a trick in which the magician does not touch the cards from first to last, yet a spectator produces a really magical effect without having the least idea of how he did it.

To produce the effect, pick out someone in your audience and assure him that he would make a first class magician. You hand him a pack of cards and tell him that he will do a real feat of magic entirely by himself. First have him shuffle the cards, then pick out the four aces and lay them on the table face down in a row, in any order he pleases. On each one you tell him to deal three cards face down, then to gather up the four heaps, in any order, and put them on top of the other cards. Next he is to cut the pack. The aces are thus well separated somewhere in the middle of the deck.

Instruct him then to deal the cards face up. While he is doing this you stop him and ask him in which pile he would like to have the aces if he were to deal four piles. Suppose he says, "In the third pile." You tell him to deal four hands of four cards in the regular way, face down. He turns over the third pile and to his astonishment there are the four aces. In view of the fact that he has shuffled, cut and dealt the cards himself and that you have not even touched them, you can imagine the bewildering effect of the trick.

As with so many of the best feats this one depends on a very simple principle. When your victim turns the cards face up after shuffling them, in order to take out the four aces, you have only to note the card on the bottom of the deck. Suppose it is the ten of spades. As soon as he has put the aces in a row face down, tell him to deal three cards face down on each one. Naturally he turns the pack and deals from the tops, so that the ten of spades remains the bottom card. Now you know that every fourth card below the ten of spades is an ace.

You say that in a moment or two you are going to have him deal four piles of four cards each and you ask him to choose in which pile the aces are to appear all together. Suppose he says "In the third pile." Tell him to deal the cards face up in one heap and watch for the original bottom card, the ten of spades. As soon as he has dealt this card, and one more, stop him and have him deal four hands of four cards in the regular way. Every third card is now an ace, so that when he has dealt the four hands and turns over the third one, the four aces are revealed.

If the person chooses the first heap you allow three cards to be dealt off after the original bottom card; if the choice is the second heap you stop him after two cards following the original bottom card, and if the third hand is chosen, after one card only. Of course, if he wants the fourth hand, you stop him dealing the cards face up as soon as the original bottom card appears.

In giving the spectator his instructions, you are carelessly strolling about and apparently taking no notice, but you watched how deep the cut went so that you can tell just about when the key card will be turned and be in a position to see it when it appears. You have made the very intricate(?) calculation required and stop the face up deal accordingly.

I am indebted to Mr. Harold Lloyd, a clever magician of England, (not of Hollywood) for this gem of impromptu tricks. Do it once and it will remain in your repertoire for good.

THE TORN AND RESTORED CARD, USING A BORROWED DECK

This trick, which is, I think, the first example of the application of the addition of a strange card to a pack, was devised by me many years ago. A version of it has recently been described by another writer. I take this opportunity of claiming my own. The effect is that a card chosen from a borrowed pack is destroyed and restored in a surprising way.

You have a card of your own, say the eight of hearts, of any pattern on the back, in a handy pocket. Perhaps the best plan is to have it in the left trouser pocket, face inwards. In the course of some tricks with a borrowed deck you have located in it the eight of hearts. Force this on a spectator and to give you an opportunity to secure the eight of hearts in your left hand, ask the drawer to hold the card up and let everyone see what it is. Palm your card in the left hand, the back of the card being next to the palm so that when you put the pack on your left hand that card joins it at the bottom, reversed.

Cut off half the pack and place the cut on the table. On this the spectator is invited to place his card and you drop the rest on top, being careful, of course, not to expose the reversed card on the bottom of this portion. Your card is thus the next card above the chosen one. Square the cards very slowly and openly and call attention to the fact that you do not lift the pack off the table.

Ask the name of the card selected, naturally you are not supposed to know what it is. "The eight of hearts," you say. "Very well, under these impossible conditions I will order that card to turn completely over, so that it will be face up, all the other cards remaining face down. "Eight of hearts, Allez donc." Spread the cards out with a sweep and the eight is revealed reversed.

This, in itself, is a sufficiently surprising effect but you have only just begun. Take up the cards above your eight and put them in the left hand, then draw the face up eight towards yourself out of anyone's reach, and place the rest of the pack on top of those in the left hand. The chosen card is now on the top of the pack.

The next move is to reverse this card and pass it to the middle of the pack. An easy way of doing this is to hand an envelope to be examined. While this is being done drop the left hand to your side, push off the top card against your thigh and turn it over, see page 94. Your hand is out of sight for a moment only and the turn takes a fraction of time to do. Making a casual cut, or, if you prefer it, the regular two hand pass, bring the card to the middle of the pack. This is then put in the envelope which is fastened down and placed in a spectator's pocket.

Pick up your eight of hearts and, keeping its face to the audience, tear it again and again into small fragments. Ball these up in a piece of tissue paper which you secretly exchange for a duplicate piece, balled similarly. Order the pieces to pass back to the pack and join up again. The tissue is opened and the fragments have vanished. The spectator opens the envelope and in the middle of the pack he finds the card complete and reversed.

A striking effect can be obtained by using flash paper to wrap up the paper, or you may put the pieces in an envelope and burn it, so destroying all the incriminating evidence.

Under proper conditions and when it is plainly impossible for you to have obtained a duplicate card, I know of no more effective trick than this. It is well to be prepared with a card of the ordinary size and one of bridge size.

THE NEW SPELL

Many versions of the now popular spelling trick are extant. Here is one which gives an effective climax to the trick. Briefly a card is chosen, replaced and the pack shuffled. The drawer of the card holds the pack behind his back and mentally spells the name of his card, bringing forward one card for each letter. When he reaches the last letter he brings the pack forward and his card lies face up on the top.

Any pack having been well shuffled you have a card freely chosen. In closing up the pack after the choice turn the bottom card over. (See page 93). Holding the pack so that this card is towards you, under-cut about three-quarters of the cards and begin and overhand shuffle. At the same time advance your hands towards the spectator, asking him to replace his card. As he goes to do this, pause in your shuffle allowing the card to be placed on top of those in your left hand and at once drop the rest of the pack on it. The reversed card is thus brought on top of the chosen card.

Square the deck up carefully and openly, showing all sides, so that it is plain there is no break, jog or crimp, but do not mention any of these artifices. Proceed again to an overhand shuffle. You know just about where the reversed card is and when the shuffle comes within a few cards of it, run the cards off singly. You are standing with your right side to the front so that when the reversed card shows up it is faced towards you and is not visible to the audience. Give this card a more vigorous flick with your thumb and let it fall to the floor. Drop all the rest of the cards from your right hand on those in the left.

The chosen card is now on top of the pack. As you stoop to pick up the fallen card, rest your left hand against your thigh, with the thumb push out the top card and deftly reverse it. In the meantime you have picked up the card from the floor with the right hand and, holding it up you inquire if it is the card selected. The answer being, of course, "No", replace it in the pack, which you are careful to hold with the bottom card facing the front.

The chosen card is now facing you so you know what it is. Remark, "I want to show you that the card is not at or near the top or the bottom of the pack, but just where chance has chosen to put it." Holding the pack with the bottom card facing the audience run cards singly off the bottom into the left hand. As you do so spell mentally the name of the card, taking a card for each letter. When you reach, and have taken off, a card for the last letter, pause and ask the drawer if he has seen his card. He says "No", and you drop the rest of the pack in front of those you have just run off, thus bringing them above the reversed chosen card and putting it in position for being spelt out.

Run off a few more cards from the bottom and again ask if the card has been seen. A negative reply is again made, so you drop the pack behind these last cards keeping them at the bottom. Next turn the pack over, take off and spread seven or eight of the top cards, ask the same question and again the answer is "No". You have already shown these last cards, but, barefaced as the procedure looks, I have never had it questioned.

Square up the pack and hand it to the drawer of the card, telling him to hold it behind his back, mentally spell the name of his card and bring forward one card for each letter from the top. Explain this carefully so that he will spell the name exactly as you have arranged for. He does this and when he comes to the last letter and brings a card forward, he naturally asks, "Well, what next?"

Ask him to name his card and then have him bring the pack forward. He does so and there is his card on the top of the pack staring him in the face.

It will be noted that the method for controlling the card and the other necessary manipulations have been worked out with the idea of placing the trick within the reach of the tyro. The skilled card worker will use his own pet moves to bring about the effect.

THE AUTOMATIC SPELLER

This trick makes a good follow-up for the preceding feat. Assert that the spelling process is entirely automatic, that the cards arrange themselves without any interference whatever from you. To prove this have a spectator shuffle the deck to his own satisfaction and tell him that from first to last you will not touch the cards. Let him turn the deck, after the shuffle, and run over the faces of the cards so that he can see for himself they are well mixed. At the same time you make a mental note of the bottom card.

Instruct him to put out three piles of six cards each, face up on the table. He will probably take the cards from the bottom of the pack as it lies face up in his hands. If he does, dismiss the card you just noted from your mind and note the bottom card of those remaining after the heaps have been dealt. The rest of the pack is laid aside face downward. It is the bottom card of this portion that you have just noted, this is your key card. Don't forget it.

If, however, he turns the pack over and deals the three heaps of six cards from the top, then the bottom card of the pack, which you have already noted, will be the key card.

In either case tell him to choose mentally one of the heaps. Turn away and instruct him to turn the piles face down, then to take any card from the pile he mentally selected, look at it; commit it to memory and place it on top of either of the other heaps. He is then to put the remaining cards of the pile he chose, mixing them first if he pleases, on top of his card and finally to take the last heap, shuffle it and put it on top of the other two. The resulting pile you tell him to place on top of the rest of the deck and cut the pack thus reassembled. At this point you turn round and see that a complete, regular cut is made.

You will readily follow the subtlety of the procedure so far. Five cards and then six more have been put on top of the chosen card and the cut has brought your key card immediately above these eleven cards. It follows that if the pack is again cut to bring the key card to the bottom, the chosen card will be the twelfth card from the top, ready to be spelt out as usual. But to the uninitiated the selected card has been utterly lost in the deck and there would seem to be no way of finding it other than to have it named and the deck searched for it. Make a great point of this before going any further.

To prove how thoroughly the cards have been mixed you have the spectator deal them out from the top face up. You are carelessly strolling about, apparently taking no note of the cards, but you know just about when your key card will appear and when it falls you stop the deal with the remark that everybody should be quite satisfied that he shuffled the cards very thoroughly. Tell him to turn the cards just dealt face down and place them under the rest in his hand. You now have the chosen card twelfth from the top.

Ask the name of the selected card. Tell the spectator to concentrate deeply on that card, to give the deck a little shake to help the cards rearrange themselves automatically, and so on. Then tell him to spell out the name of his card, taking off a card for each letter and, to his astonishment his card is turned at the end of the spelling.

But, you will pertinently remark, every card in the pack is not spelled with twelve letters. That is quite true and since you cannot manipulate the cards in any way, the sole effect depending on your not touching the cards from first to last, you will have to "manipulate" the spelling. The majority of the cards, by adding the word "of" can be spelled with either eleven or twelve letters. Thus "Four of Hearts", twelve letters, "Two of Spades", eleven letters. In the case of twelve letter cards the card must be turned on the last letter, for eleven letter cards have the card following the last letter turned up.

For the 3, 7, 8 and queen of hearts and spades simply omit the word "of" and turn the twelfth card; spell the suit first.

For diamonds proceed thus: if the card is a 3, 7, 8 or queen you say, "What was the suit? Diamond? All right, spell that out." That disposes of seven cards, so you have five left for the spots or queen, the card appears and is turned on the last letter.

For the ace, 2, 6 and 10 of diamonds you must add the "s" so making eleven letters and turn next card, and the same treatment with the 4, 5, 9, jack and king will bring the card out on the eleventh letter.

All the club cards come out at 11 or 12 letters with the exception of the ace, 2, 6 and ten. With these you must add "an" or "a". Thus for the ace you will at once say, "You chose an ace of clubs?" Very well, spell that out." The ace appears on the last letter. The addition of the word "a" to the other three will give eleven letters and turning the card following will make all right. A little practice will make the right method of spelling almost automatic.

I am indebted to Mr. Mihlon Clayton, of Asbury Park, for this clever arrangement.

A REVERSAL OF FORM

In this method of producing this popular effect an apparently three-fold reversal is obtained by very simple means. First a wrong card is found reversed, this is replaced and rights itself, finally, after the pack has been spread and shown in order, the chosen card turns over at command.

You can use any pack and allow anyone to shuffle it as he pleases. Spread the pack for the free choice of any card and in closing the spread, reverse the two bottom cards. Have the spectator show his card to everyone and so get an opportunity to turn the pack over, bringing the two reversed cards uppermost.

Cut the pack about the middle, slipping the top reversed card on to the lower part of the cut, thus hiding the fact that the other cards are face up. Have the chosen card replaced on this lower part and at once drop the rest of the pack on it. Carefully square the cards to show that the card is really lost in the middle. Drop the left hand carelessly to your side with the pack held in it and take a pencil from your pocket with the right hand, give this to the drawer asking him to make a note of his card. You take advantage of this favorable moment to reverse the top card by pressing the pack against your thigh (See Fig. 18) pushing the card off and deftly turning it over. Bring the pack back into view with the back of the left hand uppermost. All the cards are now facing the same way except the two in the middle.

Announce that the chosen card will turn over at your command. Riffle the cards and spring them from hand to hand saying that the turn will be visible. The spectators get a glimpse of a reversed card and naturally infer that it actually turned at that moment. Run through the cards and show that one card has reversed itself, there really are two cards but you hold them well squared so that there can be no suspicion that the chosen card is under the visible one. The spectator tells you that the card you are showing is not his card.

Pretend to be incredulous and have him refer to his note. He insists you are wrong, so lift off the two cards as one, and, holding the pack in the left hand, backs of the cards to the front, let it fall slightly open at a point about ten cards from the bottom. Holding the two cards also with backs to the audience, make a motion of replacing the card in the break. Really let the card you have just shown drop and retain the other, the chosen card. To the audience it appears that you have simply changed your mind and still hold the card they just saw.

"Wait a moment," you say, "This card should go back as it was and learn a lesson." So, still holding the card with its back to the audience, turn the pack round and insert it reversed. Thus you have actually reversed the chosen card under the very noses of the spectators, but they have no suspicion of the real state of affairs. Insert the card so that it will be a few cards above the other card which you placed about ten cards from the bottom.

"Now," you continue, "I shall have that card right itself so that we can begin the trick over again without its interference. Over you go." Riffle the pack and turn it over, then, running through the first few cards from the bottom, show that the card you had just before shown, is now facing the same way as the rest of the pack. A little further on in the pack, the chosen card is lying reversed and you are careful not to expose it. Boldly spread the whole pack, showing that all the cards are face up. This is perfectly safe if you make an even spread. Only the white margin of the reversed card will show. For this reason only, cards with white margins should be used in all reversed card effects. Cards with solid back patterns, such as Steam Boats are not safe for these effects as the slightest spread will betray the artifice used.

Hand the pack to the person who drew the card and, while he holds it tightly, order his card to reverse itself. As this has already been done, you can make the command as impressive as you like, Have your victim name his card and spread the pack face down. He finds his card face up.

Or you may have the pack spread with the face up. One card is seen to be face down. Then you have him name his card for the first time. He turns the reversed card over. It is his card.

ROYAL MARRIAGES

The plot of this trick is taken from Hofzinser's Card Conjuring, p. 127, "The Queen of Hearts." Hofzinser's routine requires the use of specially prepared cards but a similar effect can be obtained with any deck in this manner.

After the pack has been shuffled by a spectator, take it and running through it, with the faces of the cards towards yourself, take out the four Kings and the Queen of Hearts, putting them face up on the table. At the same time secretly place the other three

Queens on the bottom, the Queen of Clubs becoming the bottom card, next above it the Queen of Diamonds and next above that the Queen of Spades.

The story runs to the effect that four of your friends, represented by the four Kings, all fell in love with the same girl, whose part is to be taken by the Queen of Hearts. "Not being able to make up her mind," you say, "As to which one she preferred and becoming rather fed up with the protestations of the love-sick swains, the lady decided to take a vacation."

Place the Kings on top of the deck in the order—Hearts, Clubs, Diamonds, Spades. The King of Hearts being the top card.

Make the pass bringing the Kings to the middle and hold the break. With the right thumb at the rear end of the deck, lift the first two Kings and cut the deck at that point. Request a spectator to put the Queen of Hearts on the lower portion, i. e. on the King of Diamonds. Replace the cut, letting the two Kings drop back on the lower portion and insert the tip of the left little finger above them. Make the pass bringing the Kings again to the top but this time with the Queen of Hearts between the King of Clubs and the King of Diamonds, that is, third from the top, the other three Queens remaining on the bottom of the deck.

"In spite of her absence," you continue, "The four friends thought of her with even greater constancy. Tired of the constant babbling of his friends the King of Hearts decided to go off by himself, anywhere to get away from them."

Push the top card over the side of the pack with the left thumb and lever it face up with the right hand, brought up from below, by striking the right hand side of the card with the upper side of the right forefinger.

Show the King of Hearts and turn it face down again in the same way. Take it off the deck and throw it face up on the table to one side.

Turn the next card, the King of Clubs, face up in the same way.

"The second friend thought of her day and night until his whole personality was identical with hers."

Push the King of Clubs and the next card, the Queen of Hearts, over the side of the pack and execute the New Top Change, Fig. 8 & 9, bringing the Queen of Hearts on top. At the word "identical" turn the top card face up and show the Queen of Hearts. In turning this card face down again, execute the sleight bringing the King of Clubs on top.

"I put the lady down over here."

Take off the top card (King of Clubs) and place it face down on the table. As far as the audience is concerned, this card is really the Queen of Hearts, so be careful not to expose its face. Make the double lift, i. e. turn the two top cards as one, and show the King of Diamonds. Then turn both as one card, face down.

"The third friend did not fare much better. He too thought of nothing else but his lady love until he completely lost his head."

Turn the top card and again show the Queen of Hearts. Push this card and the next one over the side of the deck and again execute the New Top Change bringing the King of Diamonds on top of the Queen of Hearts.

"I will place this Queen of Hearts here also."

Put the top card, (The King of Diamonds) face down beside the other supposed Queen. Make the double lift and show the King of Spades.

"The fourth friend tried to forget the lady but in vain."

Turn the two cards, as one, face down. "Her image appeared to him at every moment of the day."

Turn the top card and show the Queen of Hearts. Once more execute the New Change, take off the King of Spades and put it face downwards beside the other two supposed Queens, saying, "I will put this Queen on the table with the other two.

"Let us give these love-lorn friends a little time to come to their senses."

Execute the One Hand Top Palm, palming the Queen of Hearts in the right hand as you put the deck down. At once, place this hand squarely on the King of Hearts, draw it off the table towards yourself, adding the Queen to it and, keeping the two well covered, place them together in your left upper vest pocket. Push the rear card well down and let about one-third of the other protrude, the back being outwards.

"Time heals all wounds and before a year had gone by the intoxication of their love was gone, their heads were clear and the lady of their hearts clean forgotten."

Turn over the supposed Queens and show the three Kings.

"We read in the Bible: "It is not good for man to live alone," so after a while each of my friends seriously considered the advisability of taking a better half. This time instead of trusting to the vagaries of the Goddess of Love they decided to let chance provide a suitable companion for each. Let us create such a chance for each of these three cards."

Take up the pack and freely shuffle off about two-thirds of the cards by the overhand method, injog one card and throw the balance on top. The three Queens, originally on the bottom, will now be just above the jogged card. Insert the tip of the left little finger above the jog and hold a break there.

Hand the King of Clubs to a lady and request her to push the card into the pack, anywhere she pleases, as you riffle the ends of the cards. Riffle rather slowly so that there will be no danger of the card being inserted above the break. It must go in amongst the lower two-thirds of the deck. Fig. 21.

Push the card in about half its length, at the same time turning the pack upright. With the right thumb push the cards above the break, held by the left little finger, until the top of the packet is flush with the top of the inserted card. Draw them upward free from the pack with the right hand.

Turn the packet face down and place it between the left thumb and first and second fingers. Fig. 22.

Draw out the King of Clubs, show it and throw it face up on the table. Draw out the card next to it, the Queen of Clubs, and without showing its face, put it face down on the King of Clubs.

Replace the packet on the rest of the cards, being careful not to expose the Queen of Diamonds, now the bottom card of the packet, and again hold a break with the little finger. In exactly the same way force the Queen of Diamonds and the Queen of Spades, putting them face down on the face up Kings. Hand the pack to a spectator to be thoroughly shuffled.

Turn over the three Queens and show that chance has arranged three happy marriages. "But we have still to settle the King of Hearts, it would not be fair to leave him without a partner." Take that card from your vest pocket but in so doing draw up the other card with the thumb and hold the two cards as one in the right hand. Take the shuffled deck with your left hand, request a spectator to lift a corner at any point, insert the two cards there, as one, and pull them through the deck from the other side. Nothing appears to have happened so you hand the deck to the spectator and ask him to take out the Queen of Hearts to pair off the remaining King. He reports that the Queen of Hearts is not in the pack.

"This King evidently knew what he wanted," you say, and you separate the two cards, opening them bookwise and showing the faces of the King and Queen of Hearts.

AN EFFECTIVE POKER DEAL

Nothing in card magic seems to impress the layman so much as the apparent ability to deal good poker hands at will. Here is an easy way to gain such a reputation.

Either beforehand, or in the course of other tricks, secretly get a royal flush,—ten, Jack, Queen, King, Ace—of any suit but Spades, to the top of the deck. The five cards may be in any order. False shuffle several times, retaining the five cards on the top and finally undercut about half the deck, jog one card and shuffle off. Cut at the jog and complete the cut, bringing the five cards again to the top of the deck. Hand the deck to a spectator and ask him to deal five Poker hands, face down, of course. This, you explain, is merely to prove that the pack has been well shuffled and that the hands will prove, most likely to be of low value.

The spectator deals five hands and naturally the first card of each hand will be one of the set-up. Pick up the hands one by one, showing the poker value of each but covering the suit of the first card as much as possible. Drop each hand face down on the balance of the deck, carefully keeping the first cards in position, and the pack will then be set to give the dealer the royal flush.

Remarking to the spectator about his being lucky or unlucky, according to the value of the hands he dealt, maintain that no luck can stand up against skill. Undertake to give an exhibition of stacking cards as used by gamblers. The hand being already set up you have merely to give as convincing a display of false shuffling and cutting as you are capable of. Deal the five hands and show that you have dealt yourself a royal flush. The reason for not using the Spade suit is that the Ace of Spades is so conspicuous that its reappearance in the final hand might be noticed and so give a clue to the secret.

With but little more trouble the trick can be made still stronger. In setting up the cards for the royal flush run four spot cards of the same value under them. In the final deal these four cards will be in the hand next to the dealer and you explain that the player in that position is to represent the "Sucker" who is to be taken to the cleaners. Invite a spectator to take that hand, and show the other three; they will probably be of small value. Let him go as far as he likes to bet, in fun, of course. The final show down gives you a royal flush against fours.

TWO CARD CONTROL

AUDLEY WALSH

Many card manipulators get a greater thrill by fooling the other fellow than by a regular performance before an audience. The following subtle arrangement by Mr. Audley Walsh, has puzzled many magicians. The effect is that two cards, openly put in widely different parts of the deck are instantly located by a simple cut.

The trick can be done with any deck and under any conditions. It depends on a subtle use of the bridge and the Charlier Pass. The routine is as follows:

Hand the deck to a spectator to be shuffled. Take it back and spring the cards from the right to the left, thus putting a downward bend at the ends of the cards. Square the pack and seizing it between the right fingers at the outer end and the thumb at the inner end, bend up and riffle about one-half of the cards, calling attention to the fact that they have been well mixed as you show the faces. The pack, if looked at sideways, would now have this appearance: Fig. 23.

The illustration is exaggerated for clearness sake, the actual bends should be much smaller.

Turn over the top card, show it and name it, say it is the Five of Spades. Replace it face down on top. With the right fingers and thumb draw out the bottom card and turning it face up, show it and name it also. Let us suppose that this card is the Jack of Diamonds. As you do this, raising the right hand with the card and directing your whole attention to it, drop the left hand slightly and make the Charlier Pass, but do not let the packets fall quite together. Hold the original bottom packet back a little with the left thumb. Fig. 24.

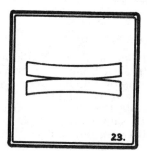

Remarking that you will put the card, the Jack of Diamonds, in the middle of the pack, place it on top of the now lower packet, that is, on top of the original top card, the Five of Spades, allowing it to protrude a little at the outer end and square the two packets.

Take up the top card, now an indifferent card, calling it the Five of Spades, but not showing its face, and insert it in the pack somewhere near the bottom. Let this card also protrude slightly from the end of the deck. Call attention to the fact that the two cards are well separated, push them flush with the other cards, and square the deck very openly. The pack if looked at sideways will look like this: Fig. 25.

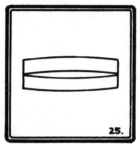

The Five of Spades will be the top card of the lower packet and the Jack of Diamonds the lowest card of the upper. By simply finding the opening of the bridge, a process that becomes practically automatic, dividing the pack at that point with the tip of the left thumb and making the Charlier Pass, the two cards return to their original positions at the top and bottom. Destroy the bridge with a riffle and there is no clue left to disclose the secret of the manipulation.

Or, you may finish by taking any card as a locator and, dividing the pack at the bridge with the left thumb, thrust the locator into the deck at that point. Square up openly and hand the deck to a spectator. He finds the locator card between the two cards that had, apparently been so fairly and widely separated. The trick must be worked smartly, the victim being given no time to notice that the face of the top card is not shown when it is thrust into the deck. In Mr. Walsh's skilful hands the feat is invariably successful.

CARD IN POCKET

DR. JACK DALEY'S VERSION

There have been many variations of C. O. Williams' subtle trick—"The Card in the Pocket". Dr. Jack Daley, of New York City, who has many ingenious tricks to his credit, has arranged a very clever application of the principle. As in the original trick, a spectator is invited to think of a number and then note the card that lies at that number from the top of a well shuffled pack. The usual suggestion of the choice of a number between one and ten has become somewhat shopworn, a better plan is to ask the spectator to think of his favorite hour. This restricts the range of the choice, avoids loss of time in counting and dealing the cards and gives an opportunity for some amusing patter. You may say that if he is addicted to early rising, six o'clock may be his choice, or the breakfast hour, eight, may appeal to him more. An Amos and Andy fan would choose seven o'clock, while an Englishman would plump for his inevitable afternoon tea hour, four o'clock, and so on.

Hand the deck to the spectator to shuffle and when he has fixed on his favorite hour, take the pack and holding it upright, faces of the cards towards him, count off the cards one by one, beginning with the top card, and saying, "One o'clock, two o'clock, etc.," asking him to note and memorize the card that appears at the hour he has mentally selected. Turn your head away as this is being done to avoid any suspicion of your getting any clue from the person's expression.

Replace the twelve cards on the top of the pack and shuffle overhand thus: undercut about two-thirds of the deck, run one card, injog the next and shuffle off. Repeat by making a break at the job, shuffle off the cards above and throw the cards below the break on the top intact. The chosen card will now be placed one card lower than its original position. Execute as thorough a series of false shuffles and cuts as you have at your command, finally leaving the thirteen cards on top intact.

Remarking that it would be a very wonderful thing if the spectator's card had been shuffled back to the same position it first held, you ask what hour was thought of. Suppose it was six, deal off five cards face down and the sixth face up to one side. It is, of course an indifferent card, the chosen card now being on top of the cards in your left hand. Take these cards with the right hand, fingers at the outer end, thumb at the inner end and drop them on the cards just dealt face down, at the same moment palm the top card by the One Hand Top Palm, (C. M. No. 1, p. 2).

Let the spectator pick up the cards and shuffle them. As he does this put your right hand in trousers pocket, leave the card there and then with left hand take handkerchief from left pocket, use it naturally and replace it. Take the pack from the spectator and spread the cards from left to right face down on the table. Instruct the spectator to think intently of his card and slowly run his left hand, forefinger extended, over the line of cards; whenever he feels an impulse he is to drop his hand and let the forefinger rest on one card. This done, draw out the card he touched, pick it up, keeping it face down, and put it in your right trouser pocket, but as your hand enters the pocket, palm the card. Gather up the cards by placing that hand flat on the right hand end of the line and sweeping it to the left. This action completely covers the addition of the palmed card to the deck, which you at once hand to the spectator.

Recapitulate what has been done—an hour thought of, a card at that number noted in a freely shuffled deck and finally a card selected from the face down deck by the spectator himself after he had again shuffled the cards. Tell him to run through the deck and take out his card. He cannot find it. Take the card from your pocket and place it face down on the table. The person names his card. Turn over the card and show that he has found that very card himself.

EVERYWHERE AND NOWHERE

This is one of the most effective card tricks ever devised. The reason that it is so seldom seen is probably because the explanations given in the textbooks are unnecessarily complicated and give the trick the appearance of being very difficult. The moves in the routine that follows have been arranged to simplify the procedure as much as possible.

The only requirements are—a small stand or card easel or, failing that, three glasses, against which to stand cards for display, an ordinary deck of cards with two extra duplicate cards, two Tens of Spades for example. Any card can be used but the black suits are preferable if the feat is to be performed before a large audience since the spots stand out so much more plainly under artificial light. Let us suppose that Tens of Spades are used, place all three on top of the deck. Begin by shuffling the deck overhand in this manner—undercut about three-quarters of the deck, injog the first card and shuffle off. Ask a spectator to draw a card, insert the tip of the left little finger below the jogged card and, spreading the pack, force one of the three Tens. This is much easier and more natural than making the pass to bring the Tens to the middle. The shuffle, being quite genuine as far as the cards actually shuffled are concerned, tends to throw the spectator off his guard and renders the force easier. In any case there should be no difficulty in forcing one of the three Tens.

As the spectator notes his card, close up the deck and insert the tip of the left little finger above the two remaining Tens. Hold the deck in right hand, fingers at the outer end, the thumb at the inner end, holding the break. As you ask the spectator to replace his card allow a few cards to drop from the bottom of the deck on to your left palm, then a few more, finally let drop all the cards below the break and hold the left hand out to receive the chosen card which is thus returned on top of the other two Tens. Make the pass, or better, bring the Tens to the top by means of the Pass Substitute No. 1 (see p. 91) .

It is necessary now to place the Tens so that one shall be next to the bottom card, one on top of the deck and the third one third from the top. To do this the simplest way, grasp the pack with the right hand as for an overhand shuffle, press firmly on the top and bottom cards with the fingers and thumb of the left hand and lift all the cards but these two with the right hand. The top card, the first Ten, will fall on the bottom card and you drop the cards from the right hand on top of them, thus placing the first Ten next to the bottom. Do this casually, while talking, then as if having changed your mind as to the manner of shuffling, split the deck in half and riffle shuffle. Let the two lowest cards in the left hand packet fall first, then execute a genuine riffle until the top cards of the packets are reached. Hold back the top card of the left hand packet and let it fall between the two top cards of the right hand packet, i. e. between the other two Tens. The three cards are now in the position required—one on the top, one third from the top and the last next to the bottom card.

The usual patter runs to the effect that by means of a scientific system a card can be found in a shuffled deck in not more than three trials. "The most likely position," you say, "Is the top of the pack." Make a double lift and show the second card.

"Is this............................of.......................your card?"

"No."

"Then I'll put it here on the table out of the way." Turn the two cards down, as one, take off the top card, the first Ten of Spades, and put it face down on the table or easel, or stand it upright against one of the glasses.

"The next likely position is on the bottom. Here is your card, the............................of............................" Say this confidently as if sure of its being right and hold the pack upright in the left hand, the bottom card facing the audience.

"What? Wrong again? Then I must put this card with the other one." Drop the left hand and by means of the Glide draw out the second Ten of Spades and put it beside the first. Now shuffle overhand by first running one card, then drop about half the deck on it, injog one card and shuffle off. The last Ten being the next card below the jogged card, make a break at that point with the right thumb at the inner end of the deck, separate the next two cards, Ten of Spades and an indifferent card, from the rest and push them forward, as one card, till they protrude from the outer end of the deck for about an inch. Turn the pack upright and with the right hand, thumb at rear and fingers in front, pull the two cards up for about three-quarters of their length above the deck. Assert now with the utmost confidence that you have succeeded.

"I have only one more chance and as my system has never failed yet this............................of...................simply must be your card. No again? You are sure? Pardon me, but did any one else see the chosen card? Oh, excuse me. I don't doubt you for a moment, but it is such an extraordinary thing for the trick to fail I thought you might have made a mistake. This is not your card." The more bewildered and anxious you can appear to be, the better the final effect. Drop the left hand, push the lower of the two cards flush with the pack, draw out the upper card, a Ten of Spades, and put it with the other two on the table.

"I must finish the trick somehow. You all say that not one of these cards (point to the easel or the glasses) is your card? Very well. May I ask you what was the card you chose? The Ten of Spades? Do you think it would be possible for me to make you see any one of these cards as the Ten of Spades? No? Let us try. Which one shall I take? The middle card?"

Take that card and hold it with its back to the audience.

"Of course it isn't really a Ten of Spades, but it will appear so to you."

Wave your hands in pretended hypnotic passes, then turn the card face out.

"You all see it as the Ten of Spades? Very well, I will replace it here."

Make the bottom change in the swing towards the table and put the indifferent card down face inwards.

"You are still sceptical? Let me prove that you are all under hypnotic influence. Of these two which would you like to see as the Ten of Spades? This one? Very well."

Repeat the same business and again change the card for an indifferent one by the bottom change, placing this card down with the first.

"One card only is left. You will see this also as a Ten of Spades."

Show the card as before, but this time it must be changed by the top change. Show the card upright, holding it with fingers on top end, thumb on the lower. The left hand holds the deck close to the body about waist high, as you say:

"Of course the card is not a Ten of Spades. The real Ten is here in the deck."

Drop the right hand bringing the card on top of the deck and at the same moment push the top card of the deck over to the right. Release the Ten of Spades from the right hand and grip this top card in exactly the same way. A moment later the left thumb pulls the Ten squarely on to the pack and moves away, the right hand remaining stationary. Finally place the indifferent card with the other two.

"Let me give you further proof. You see this top card?"

Make the double lift and show an indifferent card. Name it and turn the two cards, as one, face down. Take off the top card, a Ten of Spades, and after more hypnotic passes turn its face to the spectators.

"Now you see it as the Ten of Spades." Replace it on top. Wave your hands again.

"Now look at the bottom card. It also is the Ten of Spades."

Hold the pack upright and show the Ten on the bottom. Under cover of this surprise make the pass and hold a break with the right thumb between the two packets. Show the pack upright in the right hand, bottom card facing the audience, an indifferent card is now seen to be there.

"It is all an optical illusion. The cards are not really Tens of Spades. They only appear so."

Place the pack in the left hand and slip the tip of the left little finger into the break. Lift off the top card and show it is an indifferent card now.

"But when I put you under the influence you can see the Ten of Spades only, look."

Cut the pack at the break and hold the top portion upright, a Ten of Spades again faces the audience. Insert the tip of the left little finger under the top card of the lower packet, i. e., the third Ten. Replace the top packet and make the pass, bringing the three Tens to the bottom. Riffle off the inner ends of these three cards and insert the tip of the left little finger between them and the rest of the cards, and hold the deck in position to execute the bottom palm. (Erdnase, p. 86.)

"I know exactly what you all suspect, that I have been trying to mislead you and that all the cards are Tens of Spades. I wouldn't do anything as barefaced as that for worlds. Look! This card is not a Ten."

Palm the three Tens in the left hand and at once turn the first card on the table face out. "Nor this," turn the next, "and this last one is not a Ten either" Turn it also.

"You see there is not a single Ten of Spades in the deck."

Spread the cards face up on the table with a flourish turning your right side to the audience as you do so and slipping the three palmed cards into your left trousers pocket at the same moment.

"In fact knowing that card is an unlucky one for my trick, I put it in my pocket before I began. Here it is."

Thrust your left hand into your pocket, bring out one of the three Tens and thrown it on the table.

Smoothly executed and well acted the feat has an extraordinary effect. It is one of the few card tricks suitable for performance before the largest or the smallest audiences. Paul Rosini, the Philadelphia prestidigitateur, makes a feature of the trick and in his hands it is a masterpiece.

A very good plan for displaying the three cards when performing the trick in a parlor, is to take a large thick book, stand it upright and insert the cards as shown in the illustration. This is another idea of Dr. Jack Daley's who also makes a specialty of the trick. In his hands it leaves nothing to be desired.

2. USING A SHORT CARD

The use of a short card makes the placing of the three cards in position very easy. Put the short card on top of the pack with the three special cards following. Undercut about half the deck and shuffle overhand. Break the deck at the short and force one of the three Tens, then square the deck openly, tapping all sides on the table.

For the return of the card, break the deck above the short card so that the chosen card goes on top of it. There will now be two Tens below the short card and one above it. When you break the pack to riffle shuffle include the short card in the right hand packet and let at least two cards from this portion drop first then hold back the top card and let it fall between the two top cards of the left hand packet. The three cards are then in the required positions viz. one on top one third from the top and the last one second from the bottom.

The routine then proceeds exactly as in No. 1.

3. WITH A BORROWED DECK

This routine is another example of the subtle principle of the addition to a borrowed deck of strange cards, the faces only of which are seen by the audience producing thereby an extraordinary effect. Take two cards from any deck of the same value and suit as the card you propose to use for the trick, say Tens of Spades. Apply diachylon to the backs, sufficient to make them adhere to another card when pressed against it. Put one of these in your right hand trousers pocket, back outwards, and the other in your lower left vest pocket, also back outward.

Locate the Ten of Spades in the borrowed deck and force it on a spectator. Palm the top card in your right hand and, as you ask him to hold the card up for all to see it when you turn your back, place right hand into pocket and press the palmed card on the prepared one already there. Palm out the two cards as you turn away from the audience, place them on the top of the pack and square the two cards carefully. Take the second prepared Ten from your vest pocket, put it face down on the top of the pack and slip a card from the bottom on top of it. Again square the edges of the cards and press firmly on them. Be careful to keep your elbows pressed to your sides while making these moves.

With these manufactured duplicates of the chosen card, the routine proceeds as in No. 1, up to the point at which the three cards on the table are shown as Tens of Spades. Then it is necessary to make the bottom change with the single card only. When one of the double cards is chosen exhibit it to the audience, upright, right fingers on top end and thumb on lower end. In apparently transferring it to the table take it with the left hand thumb on the back and fingers on the face card. Fig. 27.

Pull the upper card, the indifferent card, away from the right hand and at the same time slide the lower card, the stranger Ten, into the right palm. Put the indifferent card down on the table and quietly pocket the palmed card. The second double card is treated in just the same way and the fact that the deck is not used in these apparent transformations greatly increases the effect at that stage of the trick.

The feat may be concluded by showing the Ten at the bottom of the pack, then spreading the pack to show that there are no duplicates and finally turning over the three indifferent cards on the table. Or, after showing the Ten on the bottom, side slip it to the top and show it there, then pass it to the middle by the slip cut and again exhibit it. Finally palm the Ten and produce it from your pocket as having been placed there before the experiment began.

The feat in this form when done in a parlor with cards that the spectators know you have never had an opportunity of handling before, is one of the most impressive that can possibly be performed with cards.

4. WITH AN ORDINARY DECK WITHOUT DUPLICATES

Several methods have been devised for doing the trick without the aid of duplicate cards, the following is, perhaps, the best. It has the advantage of dispensing with the force, since any card may be used for the effect, but mastery of the Mexican Turn Over is necessary for its presentation.

From any deck allow free choice of a card, have it replaced, bring it to the top, palm it and offer the deck to be shuffled. The expert will use his own favorite methods to accomplish these results but the neophyte is advised to use Pass Substitute No. 1, page 91, and the One Hand Top Palm, C. M. Series, page 2. Replace the palmed card on top (see page 88).

Pattering about the trinity of affinity, the spectator, the performer and the card, giving three chances to find the card, place the deck in your right hand outside coat pocket. Take off the two top cards, as one, and bring them out with the indifferent card showing to the audience. On being told that card is not the chosen card, place the two cards, still as one, face down on the left palm.

Bring out any other card as the second chance. This, too is wrong and you put it face down on the other two cards on your left hand. Repeat the same process for the third chance, putting the card on the others but immediately palming it off again as you square the packet prior to spreading the three remaining cards fan-wise with their backs to the audience. (See Gambler's Palm p. 83.)

Remove the pack from your pocket, adding the palmed card in so doing, and put it on the table, cut and complete the cut, thus burying the card secretly returned to it. Lay the three cards face down on the table and spread them apart, the chosen card being in the middle. Suppose the middle card is now selected by a spectator, pick up one of the others and with it turn over the middle card in just the same way as when doing the Mexican Turn Over but do not make the change.

Turn the card in hand face up but hold it tilted away from the spectators so that its face is not visible to them, and with it turn the chosen card face down, this time making the change, leaving the chosen card face down in the right hand. Drop this card beside the third card and again allow a choice to be made. In the same way by means of the Mexican Turn Over each of these is shown to be the chosen card.

Take up the card and with a gesture towards the deck, make the bottom change and throw the card face down beside the other two. Finish by showing the chosen card at the bottom, then bringing it to the top by the side slip, from there to the middle by a false cut or top slip, finally palming the card. Spread the deck face up on the table and turn the three cards face up. There is no such card amongst them. Produce the chosen card from your pocket as having been placed there before you began.

THE EXPANDING AND DIMINISHING CARDS

EFFECT: The cards are expanded to nearly twice their usual size and then diminished by several stages until they vanish completely.

REQUIREMENTS: A stripper pack of Steamboats, or other cards with backs of a solid pattern, i. e. without white margins; stripped a little more deeply than usual. A giant card and a miniature card with similar backs, and a small stand against which to display these cards upright.

PREPARATION: Arrange thirty-two cards in pairs, taking cards that most resemble each other, for instance, the kings and jacks, nines and tens, and sevens and eights of each suit. Turn each alternate card round so that the narrow end of the first card will point outwards and the narrow end of the second card inwards. Fig. 28.

Thus arranged if the ends of the pack are pulled outwards and the cards fanned, the similarity of the alternate cards will give it the appearance of having been elongated. One odd card must be put on the top and the ace of diamonds must be on the bottom with the Three of Diamonds behind it. If you now take the pack in your left hand and with the right strip the reversed cards out for about three-quarters of their length you will find that by pressing tightly on the cards at the top and bottom of the packet held by the left hand, you can safely fan the elongated pack and still retain the protruding cards in position.

This order is retained throughout the trick, and the reason for an Ace being put at the bottom is that the illusion of the cards being diminished would be spoiled by the disproportionate amount of the pattern being visible at the various stages if any other card faced the audience. Thirty-two cards only are used because the full pack is too bulky for neat handling in the manipulations, unless indeed, you are fortunate enough to have a very large hand. Place an extra card, any card, in front of the Ace of Diamonds, for a reason to be given later.

The giant card you fix in a paper clip sewn on the inside of the vest in such a position that when the lower end of the card is pushed into the clip, the upper end will be just out of sight at the top of the vest. The miniature card you fix in a similar manner under the lappel of the coat on the right hand side.

THE WORKING: Let us suppose that you have worked some such trick as the "Cards up the Sleeve," or the "Three Cards Across," remark that the explanation of the mystery is that the cards are made of rubber and that by pulling and squeezing them, they can be made any size you please. Offer to show how it is done and pick up your arranged stripper deck. You will, of course, be careful to use a pack with the same backs in your preceding trick.

"You see the cards are the ordinary size," you say as you take off the odd card from the bottom . "I will put one here so that you can fully appreciate the changes in the size of the cards." Place the card upright against the stand on the table. Then spread the pack fanwise in the left hand with the backs to the spectators, you have your right side to the front. Fig. 29.

"Suppose I want the cards a little bigger. I simply pull them like this." Take the outer end of the deck in your right hand and strip the cards out about an inch. Spread the cards fanwise with the right thumb and exhibit the cards, thus enlarged, in the left hand with their backs to the front. Fig. 30. They must be firmly held between the thumb, pressing on the backs, and the fingers on the faces of the cards. Keep your left hand in motion, as if to show the enlarged cards to everyone, the point of junction between the two packets will not then be visible.

Close the fan sharply with the right hand, then strip the packets a little farther apart, this time leaving only about three-quarters of an inch of the upper packet interweaved in the lower cards. Still standing with your right side to the spectators, spread the pack in as wide a fan as possible, being careful to press down firmly with the left thumb, holding the projecting cards in position. Fig. 31.

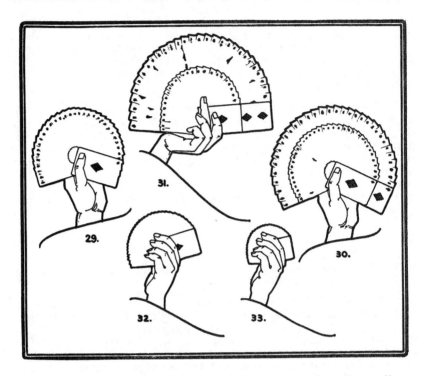

Keep the hand moving as before, then turn to face the audience direct. With the right hand at the top of the fan make a pretense of adjusting the cards which now have their faces to the front. Slip the right first finger and thumb behind the top of the fanned cards and at the same time bring the left hand back until the top of the fan is just above the opening of the vest, as if to better display the increased size of the cards. With the tips of your right thumb and forefinger seize the giant card by its upper end and, raising both hands slightly, draw it from the vest behind the fan. To facilitate this steal you should have the top button of your vest unfastened.

Slide the right hand top corner of the giant card between the two of the cards in the middle of the fan, then slowly draw it out. If the card has the same pattern as the pack, show it back and front; if not, then show the face of the card only and stand it on the table beside the card already there.

Close the fan as you say, "If I want to reduce the cards I simply squeeze them so." Cover the pack with your right hand and with a pretense of squeezing them vigorously, push the projecting cards down until a little less than half their length protrudes. Turn to the left and again spread the cards fanwise, showing their backs and keeping your hand in motion as before. (Fig. 30.)

"Another squeeze and they are back to their original size." Bring the right hand over the cards and push the projecting cards flush with the lower packet, then spread them and hold the squared up pack close to the giant card to show the reduction in size. (Fig. 29.)

"It is possible to reduce them to half the size." Bring the right hand over the pack. Make a pretence of squeezing the pack vigorously and then strike it with the half closed hand. As you do this turn to face the front, bringing the back of the left hand towards the spectators. Hold the pack in such a way that only one-half is visible above the left forefinger. Again spread the pack fanwise and the cards appear to have been reduced to half their original size. (Fig. 32.)

"With a little more pressure they can be made smaller still." You close the fan and squeezing the cards as before, push the pack a little further down in the left hand, allowing only about half an inch to protrude. Strike them several times with the half closed right hand. Spread these apparently miniature cards, Fig. 33, and, as if to display them better, bring the left hand back against the lappel of your coat. In the same way that you secured the giant card, grip the tiny card concealed there by the tips of the right thumb and first finger, and bring it out behind the fan. Draw it out from between two of the cards about the middle of the fan, show it and place it upright against the stand, beside the giant card.

"I can make the cards so very small that they will be scarcely visible. Just a squeeze and a hard tap, like this, and you can barely see them." At the word "squeeze" palm the pack in the right hand, instantly raising it about six inches, back of the hand to the front, of course, and bring it down sharply, striking the tips of the left fingers and thumb. Press the thumb and fingers together, as if holding the compressed cards with difficulty, close the lower three fingers of the right hand inwards, bending the palmed pack towards the palm, and point with the right index finger to the left hand.

Palming the pack will require a little practice ,but if the right positions are taken, there is no real difficulty in executing the move. To close the fan of the very small cards, place the right hand, held vertically, against the right side of the fan so that the first joint of the forefinger touches the top right hand corner of the fan. Close the spread by moving the right hand to the left and, the moment the pack is squared, bend the tip of the left first finger under it and propel the pack into the right hand. The instant it is palmed, raise the right hand and strike the tips of the left fingers and thumb with the heel of the hand. At the same moment turn to the left and point to the left hand.

The next move is to change over the pack from the right hand to the left. This is done as you turn to the right, bringing the left side to the front. The hands are brought together as you face front and, under cover of their backs, the change over is made, the turn to the right is continued, the right fingers and thumb being pressed together just as the left fingers and thumb were a moment before, and the left index finger is extended, pointing at the supposed tiny cards in the right hand. The transfer takes but the fraction of a second. In order to spring the pack from the right hand to the left, bend the right second finger, top joint, in behind it as you bring the right hand to meet the left. The instant the left hand secures the pack, turn your right hand upwards, palm to the front, and pretend to take the compressed cards between the tips of the first two fingers and the thumb. You should do this with an effort, as if taking something that would expand if you did not hold it tightly.

Raise the right hand with the imaginary cards and concentrate your whole attention on it. "When the cards have been squeezed as small as this," you say, "they can be easily passed up the sleeve." Snap the right fingers and open them wide, showing right hand empty. At once thrust the left hand under your coat, just above the shoulder, and push the pack well in. Then with the right hand throw your coat open and bring out the cards, holding them at the tips of the left fingers by their extreme ends, spreading them at the same time into as big a display as possible.

For the purpose of the trick it is necessary to spread the pack smartly with one movement of the right thumb across the back. The modern method of fanning the cards, by bending them as the spread is made, is not suitable.

I cannot too strongly recommend the student to devote the time necessary to master this most charming of all manipulative feats with cards.

FLOURISHES

ONE HAND SHUFFLES

1. VARIATION OF THE CHARLIER PASS

Hold the pack in the usual way for the Charlier pass, i. e., by the sides at the tips of the left thumb and second and third fingers. Fig. 34.

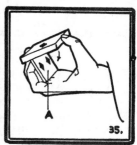

1. Release the thumb grip on a few of the lowest cards of the pack, letting them drop into the hand. Call this packet A. Fig. 35.

2. Push these cards back against the thumb with the forefinger, pressing them against the side of the thumb so firmly that they are bent a little inward, so that their upper sides just clear the inner side of the pack. Fig. 36.

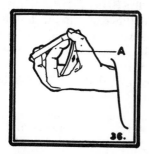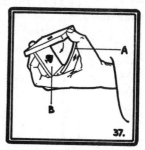

3. Release a second packet from the bottom of the deck, letting it fall into the hand. Call this packet B. Fig. 37.

4. Relax the pressure of the thumb on A and allow it to fall on B.

5. With the forefinger push B A up against the thumb, clearing the inner side of the deck and holding the cards with the thumb as before. Fig. 38.

6. Drop a third packet, C from below the pack as before. Fig. 39.

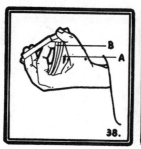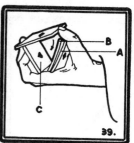

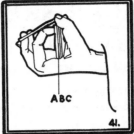

7. Release A B with the thumb and let the cards fall on C. Fig. 40.

8. With the forefinger push A B C up against the thumb. Fig. 41.

9. Drop the rest of the pack into the hand, and

10. Finally let A B C fall on top and square the deck. Fig. 42.

In executing this flourish the pack should be held with its outer end directly towards the audience and a pause of a second or two must be made after each movement. There should be no attempt at speed. If done very quickly the separate movements become indistinguishable and the audience will be unable to follow what is being done. At the proper pace the eye can follow the moves and prestige will be obtained for the actual accomplishment of a one hand shuffle.

No. 11 THREE CUT SHUFFLE

1. Hold the pack in the left hand so that it lies across the palm, upright, back resting against the side of the thumb, tip of thumb resting on the upper side and pressing down so that the pack is bent inwards a little. Fig. 43.

2. With the tip of the second finger pull down a few cards and slip the first joints of your first and third fingers under them. Fig. 44.

3. Straighten out the fingers and carry the cards outwards as in Fig. 45. They are turned over in the process.

4. With the tip of the third finger pull down a second packet and slip the first joint of the little finger under it. Straighten out these two fingers and carry these cards outwards as in Fig. 46.

5. Let the rest of the pack drop on the palm, face down, by releasing the grip of your thumb, and close your third and little fingers bringing the packet they hold on top. Fig. 47.

6. Do the same with the packet held by the first and second fingers. Fig. 48. Square the pack.

No. 111. THE FIVE CUT SHUFFLE

1. Hold the pack upright across the left hand, pressed firmly into the fork of the thumb, bottom card facing the front, and bent inwards against the side of the thumb by pressure of its first joint which bears down hard on the upper side of the deck. Fig. 49.

2. With the first joint of the third finger pull off a small packet, A, from the face of the deck, bend the first joints of the other fingers under the packet and straighten all the fingers. Packet A will be carried outwards as in Fig. 50 and 51.

3. With the tip of the second finger pull off a second packet B. Fig. 52. Bend first joint of index finger underneath it. Straighten these fingers and carry B outwards, holding it between the first joints. Fig. 52.

4. Let a small packet, C, drop from the face of the pack flat on the hand. Fig. 53.

5. Close the first and second fingers and drop B on top of C.

6. Drop another small packet, D, from under the thumb, on top of C.

7. Close the third and fourth fingers and deposit A on top of D, B, C.

8. Drop the rest of the cards from the thumb on top of all and square the pack.

All three of these flourish shuffles can be done by both hands simultaneously, half the deck being held in each hand. Indeed, it is best to learn them by using half the pack only in the left hand. I must repeat that the moves must not be done too rapidly. I have seen them executed at such a fast pace that the onlookers could form no idea of what had really been done, with the result that an exhibition of skill which would have drawn rounds of applause from an assembly of magicians, passed off in dead silence.

IV. THE MULTIPLE CUT

Hold the pack in the left hand on its side, upright, the bottom card facing the audience, the first joint of the thumb on the outer end of the pack and the lower side of the pack resting on the palm and across it. The pack being held by the pressure of the thumb, the lower corner of the pack opposite end, held by the thumb should rest against the fleshy part of the palm, about midway between the base of the little finger and the wrist.

1. Let a few cards fall forward on to the palm from the bottom as in Fig. 54. Push the first joints of the first and little fingers under them, then straighten the fingers, as in Fig. 55, carrying the cards away and turning them face up.

2. By slightly relaxing the pressure of the thumb at the end of the pack let a second packet fall face down on to the palms as in Fig. 56.

3. Bend the fingers inward and place the cards they hold on top of the cards on the palm.

4. Grip the packet thus formed and carry it outwards by straightening the fingers as in move No. 1.

5. Drop another packet from the face of the deck and again bend the fingers inward, depositing the cards they hold, then seizing the augmented packet and carrying it away.

These movements are repeated until the cards held by the thumb are exhausted; smoothness rather than speed should be aimed at.

SERIES 5

CARD MANIPULATIONS NO. 5 By JEAN HUGARD
CONTENTS

Part I.—Sleights

1. THE HUGARD PALM

By means of this sleight cards can be palmed imperceptibly, although the bottom card of the deck remains in full view.

Hold the pack in the left hand, vertically, the bottom card facing the audience, the thumb at the middle of the upper side, lower side resting on the first joints of the middle and third fingers, the first and little fingers doubled back so that their nails rest on the back of the rear card. Fig 1.

Standing with your right side to the front bring the right hand to the pack and grip it by its lower corners with the tips of the thumb and first finger. The bottom card should be in full view over the back of the right hand, the fingers of which are held close together and bent in to the same extent as the forefinger which holds the outer corner of the pack.

At the same moment pull back the lower sides of the cards to be palmed, with the tips of the left middle and third fingers, gripping them against the backs of the left first and little fingers. Extend the left fingers downwards, thrusting the packet into the right hand, the left thumb remaining on the upper side of the pack throughout. An imperceptible contraction of the second, third and fourth fingers will hold the cards securely. Remove the left hand with a careless wave, and let your eyes follow it.

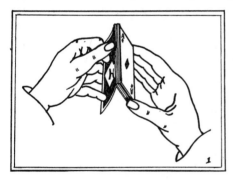

The palm can be made in a flash but there is no necessity for great speed since the move is covered by the back of the right hand. This is the cleanest method of palming yet devised for the production of fans of cards from various parts of the body. This flourish will be treated fully in a later chapter.

2. ONE HAND PALM FOR A NUMBER OF CARDS

This clean and rapid method of palming a number of cards from the top of the deck was originated by a French magician and is almost unknown here, probably because no correct description has appeared in English text books.

Hold the pack between the tips of the right fingers at the outer end and the thumb at the lower left corner. Bend the thumb a little inward so that the cards lie exactly below, and in line with, the fingers and the palm.

Bend the cards as if about to spring them from the hand and allow the inner ends of the cards to be palmed to slip from the thumb upwards into the hand where they are held by a slight additional contraction of the second, third and fourth fingers. Immediately afterwards straighten the thumb outwards, bringing the deck into view. The action takes place while transferring the deck to the left hand or putting it on the table. Fig. 2.

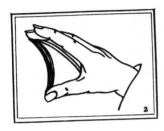

It is said that the originator of the move was able to release the cards one by one in making the palm and so could secure any desired number of cards at will. To do this requires a great deal of practice, the same result can be secured very simply by holding a break below the cards required and letting them slip in one packet.

4. THE SPRING PALM

One of the first moves that attracts the dabbler with cards, is the flourish of springing the cards fron one hand to the other. This can be turned to good use in covering a rapid and imperceptible palm of the top card.

In executing the flourish the fingers of the right hand are straightened out as the last card leaves the hand. In using the flourish to palm the top card, however, the second, third and fourth fingers are bent inward as the last cards leave the hand, the forefinger only remaining extended, and they pull the top card back into the hand. Fig. 3.

The sleight is executed with the right side of the body to the front so that the back of the hand is towards the spectator. The action is not difficult as a few trials with the cards will show.

The following tricks will serve as examples of effective use of the spring palm.

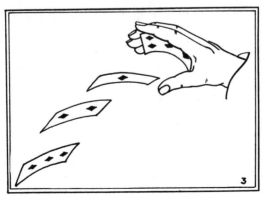

a. Introducing the Ambitious Card Trick

Have a card freely chosen, returned, and, by means of the pass, pass substitute, or your favorite method, bring it to the top. By the double lift show that the top card is not the chosen card. Let the two cards remain face up and turn the deck over. Show that the bottom card is an indifferent one also.

Holding the pack in the same position draw out the lower of the two reversed cards, showing it again, turn it over and replace it. Turn the pack again and the chosen card will be reversed second from the top.

Making some remark about the ambitious nature of the cards, have the chosen card named, execute the spring palm and it appears with startling effect facing the spectators on the top of the deck.

The palmed card can be slipped to the bottom under cover of squaring the deck, or it may be left on top of the chosen card in the action of turning that card face down. In the latter case you are ready to continue with the routine moves of the favorite "Ambitious Card" trick.

b. A "STOP" Trick

After having satisfied a spectator that his card has been lost in the deck but, in reality, having brought it to the top and kept it there, spring the cards into your left hand. Tell your victim that you will repeat the flourish and invite him to call "Stop" whenever he wishes.

Spring the cards into your left hand as before and stop the movement when the call is made. Then spring the remaining cards on to the table, palming the last card, i. e. the chosen one.

Pick up the cards from the left hand, adding the palmed card (C. M. No. 4, p. 88), and put them face down on the table, the tip of the forefinger pressing on the middle of the top card. Let the spectator name his card and show that he actually stopped you at that very card.

c. As a Force

By a slight modification of the moves in b. an easy, sure force can be made. Have the card to be forced on the top of the deck. Spring the cards into your left hand, inviting a spectator to call "Stop" whenever he wishes, then spring the remainder of the cards on to the table, palming the top card.

Take the cards from the left hand, adding the palmed card, and hand the packet to the spectator inviting him to note the card at which he stopped you.

d. The Shipwreck

For this effect it is necessary that one of the four kings be forced and after it has been replaced, and the pack shuffled, it must be on top of the pack. These moves having been made by the reader's favorite methods the next step is to borrow a hat. This, you explain is to represent a ship, the fifty-two cards the passengers and crew, and the chosen card is to be considered to be the captain.

Turn up the sweat band of the hat and put it crown downwards on the table. Holding the cards ready for the Spring Flourish, say, "The ship is all set to sail and the captain, crew and the passengers embark,"—spring the cards into the hat, palming the top card. Fig. 4. Turn the sweat band down and slip the palmed card under it. "They start their voyage, weather calm and everybody happy." Take the hat by the brim, fingers inside and thumb outside, nipping the card under sweat band and covering it with the fingers. Move the hat around.

"Soon they run into a storm, the vessel rolls, she almost turns turtle,"—shake the hat and simulate as best you can the movements of a small vessel buffeted by a storm. "Finally the captain gives the order, "Abandon Ship". Empty the cards out on the table, turning the hat upside down and shaking all the cards out. Keeping the fingers over the part of the chosen card protruding from the sweat band, show that the hat is empty. Put it on the table crown downwards, letting the chosen card slip down from under the band.

Gather up the cards and hand them to the spectator who drew a card, asking him to see if it is amongst those rescued. He cannot find it. Ask him to name it. "The King of———." You say, "Evidently since we appointed your card to be Captain he has followed

Chosen Card

4

the tradition of the sea and gone down with his ship. Will you see if it is so?"

The spectator takes up the hat and finds his card in it.

e. A Startling Transformation

Although the spring palm is not used in this feat it is included here as being perhaps the best of all tricks done with the Spring Flourish. The effect is this—a card having been freely chosen, replaced and the pack shuffled, the magician produces a wrong card. This is pushed into the deck so that about three-quarters of its length protrudes from the side. The cards are then sprung from hand to hand and the card visibly changes to the one drawn.

The method is this: Allow a card to be freely chosen and replaced. Bring it to the top by whatever means you prefer and false shuffle, leaving an indifferent card above it. Announce that you have found the card and turn the top card face up. The drawer tells you that is not his card. Execute the double lift, standing with your right side to the front and the deck almost upright on its side, to prevent exposure of the second card's face, and insert the two cards, as one, in the side of the deck. Allow about three-quarters of an inch of the length of the cards to protrude.

Announce that you will cause the card to change visibly into the correct card and have this named. Spring the cards downwards smartly into the left hand. The two cards turn over, leaving the chosen card face up and protruding from the other cards.

I must confess that until I saw this feat done perfectly I was sceptical as to its practicability. It does require some work but the change is so startling that it is well worth the effort required to master it.

4. A Flesh Grip

The loose flesh at the root of the thumb can be used to maintain a break after the pack has been cut, doing away with the necessity of inserting the tip of the left little finger, in this manner—

Pick up the cut and put it in the left hand, well down on the palm, and squeeze the left side of the packet tightly against the fleshy root of the thumb by pressing the second, third and fourth fingers against the right hand side of the cards. In putting the other half of the pack on top it will be found an easy matter to clip a fold of the skin between the two packets.

The outer ends of the cards may now be tapped perfectly square, the first joints of the left fingers are all on top of the deck so that it can be shown quite freely and the bottom ends of the cards can be tapped on the table without the least danger of losing the break. This can be found instantly by the right thumb tip by feel alone and the deck split at that point for a riffle shuffle, thus avoiding the pass; or the break can be opened a little, the tip of the left little finger inserted and the pass made in the usual way; or the pack may be picked up for an overhand shuffle, the break being held with the tip of the thumb, the cards above the break being then shuffled off and the balance thrown on top.

Again, the flesh grip can be secured after the insertion of the little finger tip, following the replacing of a chosen card. The tapping of the ends of the deck and the position of the left fingers on top will convince the most sceptical spectator that his card has really been lost in the deck.

5. THE PEEK OR GLIMPSE

This term is applied to the method of ascertaining what a given card is unknown to the spectators. The earliest description of the sleight that I have been able to find is that given by Robert Houdin in his book, "Les Secrets de la Prestitidigitation et de la Magie," published in 1868, as follows:

"You slip the little finger under the card you desire to know, then with extreme rapidity you open the pack at that point and, with a swift glance, ascertain what the card is. The necessary movement, quick as lightning, cannot possibly be perceived by the public, inasmuch as it is made while carelessly waving the hand about, and with the backs of the cards towards the spectators."

In Robert-Houdin's time there were no indices on the cards, hence to be sure of noting the card the pack had to be opened quite widely, book fashion, the upper part of the pack being gripped between the third and little fingers. With modern cards this is not necessary, the lower end of the packet being raisd by the little finger just enough to allow a glimpse of the lower index.

It must be noted particularly that your gaze must be directed at the spectators and not at the pack. In the course of a natural gesture accompanying your patter, the pack is brought in the line of vision. At that moment the index is exposed and the card noted. Fig. 6.

There are many modern methods of sighting a card. The best of which follow.

A. SIGHTING THE TOP CARD

1.   The Palm. Pass the card to the top, palm it in the right hand and give the pack to a spectator to shuffle. In so doing the card is brought directly into view. Care must be exercised in choosing the person to shuffle the deck, to avoid exposing the palmed card. The best palm to use for this method is the One Hand Palm (C. M. No. 1, p. 2). As the pack is placed on the spectator's hand the outer index of the palmed card will be visible to you just above the tip of the little finger. Fig. 7.

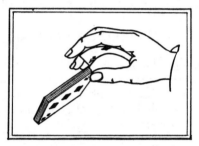

Fig. 7

2.   The Ruffle. Hold the deck upright, facing outwards, between the second, third and fourth fingers of the left hand and the first finger which is doubled back, the thumb resting on the top corner of the deck. Execute the one hand ruffle by bending the corners of the cards back and releasing them rapidly one by one, holding back the top card. Do not look at the cards as the ruffle is made but note the exposed index as you take the pack in your right hand. The ruffle may be accompanied by some such remark as this, "Your card is in the pack somewhere. Impossible for me to know just where." Fig. 8.

Fig. 8   Fig. 9

3.   The Push Down. Hold the pack in the left hand, face down, the bottom card facing the front, the left forefinger doubled back on the bottom card. With the ball of the left thumb push the top card down a little and then outwards, holding the other side of the card flush with the rest of the pack. This action will bend the middle of the card upwards and enable you to glimpse the top index easily. The sleight may be performed under cover of a wave of the hand or in tapping the lower end of the deck on the table to even it up. It is imperceptible if the bottom card faces the front squarely. Fig. 9.

Method No. 3 can be used to ascertain secretly the name of a card at any number from the top. Holding the pack in exactly the same way, thumb count the cards to the desired number, press the ball of the thumb on the corner of the packet so separated and it will be found that the index can be sighted just as with one card. Obvious as this development of No. 3 appears, it has never before been described, or even used, so far as I can ascertain.

5. Left Thumb and Lower Index. Hold the pack upright in the left hand, face down, forefinger bent over the top and the other three fingers on the back, thumb at the side of the deck but taking no part in supporting it. Tap the lower end of the pack on the table at the same moment bending up the lower left corner of the top card with the tip of the thumb. It is quite natural for one to look at the deck as it is being tapped on the table and, since the action of the thumb is covered by the pack, the sleight is imperceptible to the onlookers. Fig. 10.

Fig. 10

6. The Double Lift. This is a very subtle method. A card having been chosen, replaced and manoeuvered to the top, make a double lift and show the second card, calling its name, suppose it to be the two of clubs. Replace the two cards face down, turn the pack face up and show the bottom card, naming it also.

Turn the pack face down again and pick up the top card, holding it so that you alone can see its face, and say, "You are sure this two of clubs (or whatever the card was that was shown by the double lift) is not your card?" Take a mental note of what the card is and replace it. Turn the pack face up and repeat the question as to the bottom card. The method is a bold one, but done without hesitation, it never creates any suspicion. This principle of miscalling a card is useful in many other effects.

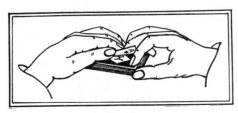

Fig. 11

7. By the Riffle Shuffle.

In executing the riffle shuffle hold the top card of the left hand packet back a moment, so getting a glimpse of it. This is a very easy method but is also easy to detect. A much better way is to push the top card of the left hand packet over the side of the deck, that is, in-jogging it at its index corner, then as you raise the corners of the packets to begin the shuffle, you note the index. Make the riffle shuffle without looking at the cards, it being a simple matter to drop the top card of the left hand packet last of all. Fig. 11.

8. Gambler's Method.

Hold the pack face down between the thumb on one side and second, third and fourth fingers on the other, first finger on the outer end. Place your right hand squarely over the cards, tips of the fingers at the outer end and the base of the thumb at the inner index corner of the top card. Turn the hands, so bringing the deck upright on its side and, with the fleshy part of the base of the thumb bend the index corner of the top card upward and note it. The action is completely under cover.

9. Hindu Shuffle.

In the course of the Hindu Shuffle (C. M. No. 1, p. 2) after the card to be sighted has been picked up under the right hand packet, let the cards fall on the left hand irregularly, turn a little to the left and tilt the packet in your right hand upwards, so that its bottom card faces you, and with it tap the inner ends of the cards on the left hand as if merely to square them. The card to be sighted is thus brought into view without arousing any suspicion since it is natural to look at the cards as you tap them square. Fig. 13.

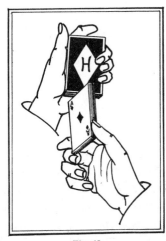

Fig. 13

It is, of course, necessary to pick up the chosen card only with the right hand. Any slight hesitation in securing it may be covered by remarking, "You will remember your card?"

10. Placing Deck on Table. Take the pack in the left hand face down then, as you turn to put it on your table, turn the hand over, bringing the deck face up and letting the ball of the thumb rest on the middle of the inner side of the deck. With the tips of the fingers push the top card to the right so that the lower index is visible for a moment just before the deck is put face down on the table. Fig. 14.

Fig. 14

This sleight can also be done in simply passing the pack from one hand to the other.

11. Overhand Shuffle. In making the first movement of the regular overhand shuffle, push the top card forward with the left thumb and sight the index, and at once pull out all the cards but the top and the bottom, thus bringing the sighted card on top of the bottom one. Shuffle off freely on these two cards. You can now show both the top and bottom cards and bring the sighted card back to the top by simply retaining the bottom card with the left fingers and shuffling off in the usual way.

B. SIGHTING THE BOTTOM CARD

1. Tilting the Pack. In offering the pack to be shuffled, hold it with the thumb below and the fingers above, slanting the outer end downwards so that a glimpse can be obtained of the outer index. This method first appeared in print in Hoffman's "Modern Magic" which was published in 1876, but since card indices had not then been introduced, the pack had to be slanted at an angle of 45 degrees to allow the full face to be visible. It is interesting to note that the method appears in a recent booklet on cards as a new discovery. Fig. 15.

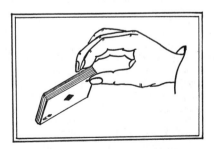

Fig. 15

2. The Rear Bend. Hold the pack face down in the left hand. Square it with the right hand, fingers at the outer end and the thumb at the rear. Separate the inner end of the bottom card from the rest with the tip of the right thumb and push the cards above it forward about half an inch. Continue the squaring movement and pick up the protruding end of the bottom card, bending it up against the rear end of the pack. The index figure will come into sight and the top of the spot will show sufficiently to identify clubs from spades and diamonds from hearts.

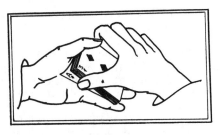

Fig. 16

3. Buckling the Card. This method is similar in effect to No. 2, but the manipulation differs. Separate the outer end of the bottom card slightly with the tip of the left forefinger, keeping the right thumb pressed against the rear end of the deck. Push the deck forward in the action of squaring the sides, causing the bottom card to buckle and so bringing the lower index into view. The action is instantaneous and completely covered.

4 Variation of No. 2. Push the rear end of the bottom card to the left with the left little finger and bend the index corner up against the side of the deck with the tip of the right thumb.

5. Turn over Flourish on Arm. A bold method of sighting the bottom card prior to forcing it, is to execute the Turn Over Flourish on the arm. (C. M. No. 2, p. 39.) Note the bottom card, no one else will, then square the deck, under-cut half, that is pull out the lower half and put it on top, slipping the little finger between the two packets.

6. Pulling back Sleeve. Take the pack from the spectator after he has shuffled it, with the right thumb underneath, fingers on top. Look him straight in the face as you ask if he is satisfied that the cards have been thoroughly mixed. Then as you extend your right arm and pull the sleeve back a little with the left hand tilt the pack and sight the index of the bottom card. Bring it to the middle by under-cutting as in No. 6.

7. Under Cover of Card Fan. Having manipulated a chosen card to the bottom of the pack, take off a dozen or so cards from the top and fan them in the right hand asking the spectator if he sees his card amongst them. Holding both hands shoulder high turn the left hand to bring the bottom card facing you and point to the fanned cards with the left forefinger, running it over the backs of the cards from left to right. You can thus note the bottom card without arousing the least suspicion.

This clever move is from T. Tucker's booklet, "What Next?"

8. Bending the Deck Inwards

a. Hold the pack upright in the right hand, thumb at the lower end, fingers at the top, the bottom card facing the audience. Squeeze the cards slightly causing them to bend inwards as in springing the cards from hand to hand. This action will bring the lower index into sight. The actual bend need be very slight and should be made while moving the hand a little from side to side as if to show the card to everyone. Fig. 17.

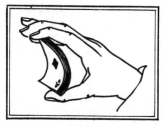

Fig. 17

b. Reading the Cards with the Fingers. The sleight is generally used in reading all the cards of a shuffled deck but the constant repetition of the moves makes it liable to detection. The best way to use it for this purpose is to glimpse the bottom card, when the pack has been returned after being shuffled, by one of the methods already described. Then hold the pack upright as in a, and with the left fingers pretend to read the card by feeling it. While doing this hold the card for a moment in the left fingers, bend the rest of the cards behind it and quickly note the index of the next one. The bend is then covered completely by the bottom card which remains perfectly straight. As many cards as desired can be read with perfect ease, each time removing the card read and glimpsing the one behind the new bottom card.

C. SIGHTING A CARD IN THE MIDDLE OF THE DECK

The classical method has already been given at the beginning of this section. Other methods follow.

1. Ruffling the Pack for Return of Card. Have the chosen card returned to the pack as you ruffle the outer ends of the cards. By squeezing the inner end of the deck you prevent the spectator from pushing the card home. Turn the deck slightly upward in transfering it to the left hand and sight the protruding index.

2. The Push Through. Proceed as in No. 1, but in squaring the deck push the protruding card through the others by turning it a little to the left, pressing on the corner with the right forefinger and then straightening it at the rear with the left little finger. The lower index can then be sighted under cover of the right hand.

3. Charlier Pass Move. In advancing to the spectator let the lower half of the pack drop as in the Charlier Pass and note the bottom card of the upper packet. At once drop this packet on the lower one in such a way that a step is formed between them. Insert the left little finger between the packets and you are ready to force the glimpsed card in the usual way.

4. Palming Half the Deck. An easy, though rather bold, plan is to palm about half the deck in the right hand and sight the bottom card of this portion while making a gesture with the right hand. Replace the palmed cards on the remainder in the left hand, slipping the tip of the left little finger betwen the two packets as you square the deck.

5. Turning Index Corner in Fan of Cards. Fan the deck widely for the selection of a card. Have a card selected and returned to the fan, but, before pushing the cards together, raise them to the spectator's eyes, asking him to take one more look at his card so that he will be sure to remember it. At the same time turn up the lower index corner of his card with the left thumb and note it.

A great advantage of this method is that the corner can be slightly crimped and, although the fan is closed quite openly and fairly and the deck immediately shuffled by the spectator, the chosen card can be easily located.

6. Index of Card Above Chosen Card. Ruffle the outer ends of the cards for the return of one chosen by a spectator, bending the cards rather far back. When the card is pushed in, note the index of the one immediately above it, close the deck and square it very openly. Later by ruffling the index corners, as in the thumb count, the sighted card can be found easily, locating the selected card next to it. The spectator may be allowed to make a short overhand shuffle with little risk of separating the two cards. This greatly strengthens the effect.

7. Sighting Card After Spectator Peeks at Index. A card having been noted by a spectator by lifting the corners of the cards and

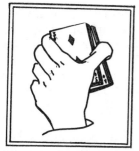

Fig. 18

looking at the index of one as in the pre-liminary to the side slip, hold a break and turn the left hand over to the right, bringing the cards face up. With the tips of the left fingers press the packet NOW BELOW the break a little to the right, bringing the lower index into view. The action is covered by the position of the hand. Fig. 18.

8. Sighting Any Card Called For. Hold the deck in the left hand face down, firmly gripped between the first joints of the second, third and fourth fingers on the bottom and the first finger doubled back on the top, the thumb rests free on the index corner. To sight any card called, bend up the corners of the cards and ruffle them, letting the corners slip one by one and noting the indexes as they pass. With a little practice any card can be found almost instantly. The late Dr. Elliott made this move, at which he was a past master, the basis of some astounding feats.

By way of conclusion to this exhaustive treatment of the peek it should be mentioned that the index of a card can be easily read when a card is covered with a handkerchief. It is only necessary to stretch the fabric a little over the top left hand corner. A very interesting feat dependent on this principle will be found on page 152.

6. The Best Overhand False Shuffle. When you have a number of cards, up to say ten or twelve, on the top of the pack and it is necessary to keep them intact in that position and yet simulate a genuine shuffle, the following is the best method yet devised for an overhand shuffle.

Hold the pack in the left hand in the usual position for an overhand shuffle. With the right second finger and thumb lift up the lower two-thirds of the pack, call this packet B, leaving the other third intact in the left hand, call this packet A.

Bring B down on A and release a small packet C from the top, at the same moment gripping A between the tip of the right third finger at the outer end and the right thumb at the inner end. Lift A together with the remaining cards of B, holding a break between the two packets. Fig. 19.

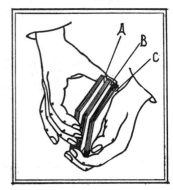

Fig. 19

Shuffle off the remaining cards of B in the usual way and, when the break is reached simply throw A on top. The action is very easy and, smoothly done, it is impossible for the onlooker to detect the least departure from a genuine shuffle.

I am indebted to Jules the Magician, of Hotel New Yorker fame, for this invaluable sleight. If the reader gets nothing else from these pages he will be well repaid for his outlay.

7. The Daley Reverse

Many methods have been devised for secretly reversing a card in the deck. Some are good, others very bad. The limit amongst the latter class was reached in a contribution to a recent magical journal. To reverse a single card the inventor used two double back cards, one short and almost a full page describing the necessary manipulations. Some people seem to delight in making their maneuvers as complicated as possible whereas the essence of good conjuring is simplicity. The following method, devised by Dr. Joseph Daley, of New York City, is the very best reversal of a single card that I have met with.

All that is necessary is to get the card to be reversed second from the top. Turn the top card over on the pack to show that the chosen card is not there. Take it and the next card, the selected one, by the lower index corner between the right thumb and forefinger, holding them as one card. Keeping the right hand stationary, with the left hand turn the deck over on the two cards to show the bottom card also. The chosen card now lies reversed and the pack being held rather low down, this reversal is completely concealed and unsuspected. In other words you reverse the pack instead of the card. Fig. 20.

If the two cards are taken cleanly, without hesitation, the operation will deceive the most observant onlooker. It is a good plan, in turning the top card, to push the next card a little off the pack and insert the little finger tip under it. In squaring the cards the grip at the lower corner can be taken without fumbling.

Fig. 20

8. Color Change

This clever variation of the "paint brush" color change is by Mr. Gerald Fulton, of Guelph, Ontario, Can.

Hold the deck in the left hand as for the color change. Call attention to the bottom card, suppose it to be the Three of Diamonds. Take any other card from the deck, the Two of Spades for example, show it and place it face to face with the three. In doing this draw off the rear card of the deck and palm it.

Let the faced card, Two of Spades, fall face up on the extended left fingers, Fig. 21, to show that the cards are still in the same position. With the right hand close the Two of Spades up against the Three of Diamonds at the same time slipping the palmed card between them by clipping its outer index corner between the second and third finger tips, so causing it to extend almost at right angles to the hand. This makes its introduction an easy matter that can be done at close quarters imperceptibly.

Now execute the double lift, again showing the three and brush it several times with the double card in the right hand, Fig. 22. Finally leave the extra card on the Three of Diamonds, thus effecting the change. The forefinger of the left hand must be placed at the outer end of the deck to act as a stop, and to ensure that the addition of the hidden card is made exactly on the three.

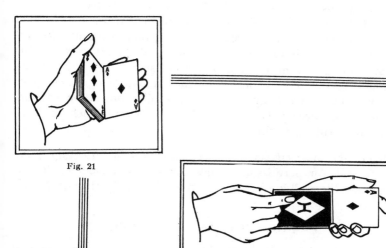

Fig. 21

Fig. 22

Part II.—The Set-Up

Tricks depending on prearranged cards are divided into two classes—those depending upon an arrangement of the whole pack in a certain order of suits and values, and those in which a few cards only are arranged in order.

For the first class there are three systems generally recognized as standard. The first, in which the cards are arranged according to the old couplet, "Eight kings threatened to save, ninety-five ladies for one sick knave," dates back over a hundred years at least and probably further back than that. The second is of more recent origin, though the date of its invention is unknown. It is popularly known as the Si Stebbins system, but in a recent pamphlet Mr. Stebbins disclaims its invention, stating that the system was given to him by one Salem Cid, and that, as far as he had been able to find out "the system is as old as the hills."

In each of these arrangements the suits follow one another in definite order throughout the pack. In neither case can the cards be handled by a spectator for it would have to be a very unobservant person who would not at once notice the set-up.

The third system originated by Louis Nicola, the English conjuror and published by him in his book in 1927, is free from this defect. To all appearance the cards are in haphazard order and it is impossible for any one to detect the arrangement without a knowledge of the key. This system is as far ahead of the other two as the modern motor car is in advance of the old stage coach. For some inscrutable reason it is neglected by most magicians. Since space will only allow for treatment of tricks depending on the prearrangement of a few cards only, consideration of the full pack must be reserved to a future booklet.

One of the most effeective tricks requiring a small set-up is the following and, for permission to describe it, I am indebted to Mr. Frank Lane, the well-known Boston magician and entertainer. He calls it—

AN INDETECTIBLE STOP TRICK

Effect: A spectator is allowed to choose a card freely from any pack. He replaces it and the pack is squared without any sleight of hand move and thoroughly shuffled. It is handed to the spectator and he deals cards from the top, stopping at any card as the spirit moves him. Noting the number of spots on this card he continues to deal that number and there he finds the card he chose. The cards before and after the one he stopped at may be examined, and indeed all the cards, without any clue being found to the solution of the trick.

Working: The explanation lies in the fact that a nine, seven, five, three and an ace, with one indifferent card between each, have been placed on top of the pack with three indifferent cards above them and the chosen card is replaced below the ace. When the pack is handed to the spectator, he is told to deal cards slowly from the top one by one. When he has dealt three cards he is invited to stop at any time he wishes. If he elects to stop then he is told to turn the top card, a nine. His card is then nine cards further down.

If, however, he continues the deal, the magician has only to keep track of the alternate cards, the seven, five, three and ace. If the spectator stops with one of these in his hand he is told to turn it face up, but if he stops while holding an indifferent card, he is to turn over the top card. In any case he is invited to look at the card preceding and the card following, and these are indifferent cards. By insisting that the deal be made slowly it is practically certain that the stop will be made before the ace is reached.

To make the necessary arrangement of the cards Mr. Lane has the drawer of the card write its name on a piece of paper, fold it and put it in his pocket. While this is being done he finds the five cards, arranges them as required and holds a break under the ace. Cutting at the break he has the chosen card replaced below it and shuffles the pack, running three indifferent cards on top of the packet set up. The trick then proceeds as described above.

Most performers will prefer to make the set-up before beginning the trick. The easiest and quickest way of doing this is to take the deck by the ends between the thumb and second and third fingers of the right hand, bottom card facing the palm of the hand, sides of the deck parallel with the floor. Put the ball of the left thumb on the top outer corner of the pack, double the left forefinger behind and let the lower side of the cards rest on the other three fingers of the left hand. By ruffling the corners with the left thumb the indices become visible. Riffle to the first nine of any suit, insert the tips of the three left fingers, press them on the face of the nine, drawing it

away downwards and deposit it on top of the deck. In this same way
a seven, five, three and an ace, of any suits, are brought to the top
one after the other.

The next step is to put an indifferent card between each of
these five and this is a simple matter. Begin an overhand shuffle by
running off the top card, an ace, into the left hand, placing it well
down into the fork of the thumb. With the tips of the left fingers
pull off the bottom card, and with the thumb draw off the top card,
the two cards falling simultaneously on the ace. Repeat this move
three times, in-jog the next card and shuffle off. Form a break at
the in-jog, shuffle to the break and throw on top. To place the three
indifferent cards on top of the set-up. To add the three indifferent
cards required it is best to riffle shuffle several times, letting the last
card from the left hand packet fall last, being careful, of course, not
to let any cards fall amongst the arranged nine. The change to the
riffle shuffle is advisable not only because it is an easy way of adding
the three cards to the top, but also to clinch the impression that the
pack is well and thoroughtly mixed.

In spreading the cards for a spectator to draw one, run them off
rather rapidly in threes till you reach the twelfth and press the tip
of the little finger on the ace, the bottom card of the set-up. Arrange
so that this point is reached before he has a chance to draw a card,
then spread the rest and allow a free choice to be made. Close up the
pack, retaining the little finger break, and, holding the pack well
down in the hand so that it will not be noticed that the cut is being
made near the top, cut at the break, have the card replaced, drop the
cut on top and square the deck very openly, tapping the sides and
ends on the table. Execute a false shuffle (p. 143) and hand the
deck to the spectator.

The denouement is then reached as already described. Care
must be taken to emphasize the slow movement in dealing and also
to bring out clearly before the card stopped at is turned, that the
cards following it and preceding it are entirely different and in
haphazard order. The effect will be found to be all that can be
desired. The trick has been treated in the fullest detail so that it
may serve as a guide in other tricks requiring the setting up of a
small number of cards.

CURIOUS COINCIDENCE

A set-up is necessary, the four nines having to be at the fourth, sixth, eigth and tenth places from the top of the pack. With the nines on the top begin an overhand shuffle by drawing off the top card into the left hand, then three times in succession pull off the top and bottom cards together on top of this, run three cards, in-jog one and shuffle off freely. Make a break at the in-jog, shuffle freely up to this and throw the balance on top. Follow this with the false shuffle on page 143 and a couple of false cuts and no layman could possibly suspect any arrangement. Put the pack on the table, let a spectator cut and ask him to touch either packet. If he touches the original top half say, "Very well, that's the packet we will use for the trick," and put it to one side.

If he touches the other one, tell him to take the cards and shuffle them. Push the remaining packet aside, saying, "Remember you had a free choice." In either case the spectator gets the lower half. After he has shuffled these cards, take them, spread them widely and allow him to make a free choice of one card. As you close the fan slip your little finger tip under the eighth card and hold a break. Cut here for the return of the card, drop the eight cards on top and square the cards very openly. False shuffle (p. 143) keeping the top nine cards intact and lay the packet down.

Now tell the spectator to take the other packet, the original top half of the deck, and deal the cards slowly on to your hand. When he has dealt a couple and has the third in his hand, tell him to stop whenever he pleases. Keep track of the nines and if he stops with one in his hand have him turn it up, but if he stops with an indifferent card in his hand take it and let him turn the next card, a nine. In either case show that the card preceding and the card following are indifferent cards.

From the top of the other packet now slowly draw off eight cards one by one. Have the chosen card named and turn it up.

Part III.—Tricks

FRANCIS CARLYLE ACES

While the broad effect of this four ace trick is the same as other versions, Mr. Francis Carlyle, the clever New York Magician, has introduced several subtleties which make it, perhaps, the best of all close-up methods. The working follows:

From any deck remove the four aces and lay them on the table. Run over the faces of the cards towards the audience to show there are no other aces, turn the pack face down in your left hand and secretly slip the tip of your little finger under the two top cards. Pick up the aces and put them face down on the top of the pack, but immediately lift them off together with the two top cards, the break allowing you to do this without any hesitation. Put the pack down and take the four aces, really six cards, face down in your left hand by the sides between the second finger and the thumb, the tip of the forefinger on the back of the packet pressing the outer end down to avoid any chance exposure of the bottom card and also to prevent anyone noticing there are more than four cards in the packet.

With the right thumb on top and fingers below, draw off the first card, turn it over and have the spectator call its name, "Ace of———". Turn it face down and push it under the packet. Remove the second in the same way and also the third ace, having each named and pushing them under the packet in turn. Take up the fourth ace, show it and have its name called and then place it back on top of the packet. By this subtle procedure you now have two indifferent cards between the first and second aces.

Drop the packet on top of the deck. Pick it up and deal four cards in a row, carelessly letting the spectator get a glimpse of the first and fourth cards, aces, but not of the second and third, which are indifferent cards. If the action so far has been made smoothly and without hesitation, the onlookers will be convinced that the aces are lying on the table, whereas there are two only, the other two being on the top of the pack.

The next step is to put three cards apparently on the first ace, but really only two. Draw the top card partly off the deck with the right hand, then another below it and a third in the same way. Grip them between the thumb and fingers by the ends and square them against the left thumb, at the same time dropping the lowest card, carrying away the two aces only and placing them on the first card you dealt on the table, that to the right of the row. In making this false count do not lift the cards from the pack, simply slide them over the side.

Immediately count off three more cards from the top of the pack, making exactly the same movements and drop the three cards on the second card in the row. Repeat this twice more and point out that you now have four packets of four cards, each with an ace at the bottom. Really the first packet consists of three aces, the second and third of four indifferent cards and the fourth has an ace at the bottom and three other cards on top of it. Touch the packets as you say this and, rather furtively, draw the first one, the three aces which should be nearest the spectator, back a little towards yourself. Invite him to touch one packet and, in nine cases out of ten he will touch this one, which is what you want him to do. If, however, he touches one of the others, continue with the old "Take or leave" method, or the "Touch two, then one," interpreting the touches to suit yourself. In any case the heap with the three aces is forced and put aside a little to your right.

Put the second and third packets on the top or bottom of the pack, taking care not to expose the bottom cards, and the fourth packet on top of the deck. You have now to secure the fourth ace and add it secretly to the other three. Mr. Carlyle does this by taking an opportune moment to side-slip the ace, the fourth card from the top, into his right palm. With his left hand he spreads the pack with a sweep face up and puts his right hand squarely on the three aces packet, so adding the fourth ace in drawing the cards towards the edge of the table, a natural way of picking up the packet, and at once throws the aces face up on the table.

The use of the side-slip may be avoided in this manner: Having replaced the three packets on the deck as described above, so that the fourth ace is the fourth card from the top, you go over what has been done, thus . . . . "You remember each ace was put on the table so" . . . . deal a card from the top . . . . "and on each ace three cards were dealt so" . . . . deal three cards on top of it . . . . "then you choose one packet and the other three returned to the pack" . . . . pick up the four cards and replace them on the pack. Their positions have been reversed and the ace is now on top. You have simply to palm this card and finish the trick as already described.

THE CARD THAT FINDS ITSELF

The feat to which the originator, Mr. Carlyle, has applied this title, is a fine addition to the list of tricks that can be done offhand with any deck. The effect is that a card is freely chosen, replaced and the pack shuffled. Another card is found reversed in the deck and the selected card is located at the position indicated by the number of its spots.

The method is simple and well covered. After having the pack shuffled by a spectator, under cover of squaring the cards, pull the top card to the bottom, reversing it in the process, and sight its top index by pulling it a littlte to the left. With an overhand shuffle run cards to the bottom, one less than the number indicated by the value of the card. Thus if the card is a seven you run six, and so on; for the court cards, jack, queen and king take the values at eleven, twelve and thirteen.

Spread the pack and allow a free selection from the cards above the reversed card, which you are careful not to expose. As the spectator notes his card, execute the Hindu shuffle, but in the first movement pull out the cards above the reversed card so that the shuffle does not disturb the set-up packet on the bottom. This is merely a blind, helping to convince the spectator that the cards are really mixed. Repeat the shuffle, this time drawing out all the cards below the top packet, telling the spectator to call "Stop" whenever he wishes to replace his card.

Stop the shuffle at the point indicated, have the card replaced and drop the balance of the deck on it, thus bringing the set-up packet immediately above it. Square the cards very openly and hand the deck to the spectator. Name the card reversed as being your indicator card and order it to reverse itself at the position above the chosen card that is indicated by its value. The deck is spread, the reversed card revealed and below it at the indicated position is the chosen card.

AN INSOLVABLE MYSTERY

This trick, very kindly given to me by Mr. Dai Vernon, the famous card expert, breaks new ground. The effect is that any pack, having been thoroughly shuffled, is placed in the performer's hand, which he holds behind his back, and is then covered with a handkerchief, in which it is securely wrapped. Any number is called by a spectator. The magician names a card. The spectator uncovers the pack, counts to the number and finds there the card called.

The method is subtle. When the pack is covered with a handkerchief, in bringing it to the front, turn the cards face up and sight the top card's index by stretching the fabric a little at that point. Hold the pack with the left forefinger below and the thumb at the index corner, ready for a riffle count. As you ask the spectator to name a number, riffle off five cards. As soon as he calls a number continue the count till you reach it. Bring your right hand over the pack and make the pass at that point under the handkerchief. Turn the deck over, under cover of wrapping it securely and hand it to the spectator. All done in a few seconds.

After much pretended mental exertion, name the card you sighted. The spectator unwraps the pack, deals cards to the number he called and finds there the card you named.

A good presentation is to have the spectator run over the faces of the first dozen or so cards after he has shuffled and your pack is turned, just glancing at the cards and not trying to remember any of them. When the deck is covered have him call a number between one and fifteen, so that the choice, you say, will be restricted to the cards he saw, really to limit the thumb count. Explain that his sublimimal consciousness has registered the positions of the cards and that altho he will not be able to recall them, you will pick up the waves of cerebration. Impress on him to make no effort to remember the card, simply to remain passive. Proceed to name the color, suit and finally the value.

The thumb count must, of course, be made noiselessly but it can be done quite deliberately since the hand is out of sight. I can recommend this as being one of the most mysterious feats possible with cards.

THE SPECTATOR BECOMES A MAGICIAN

Here is a very diverting effect obtained by the simplest possible means, the only precaution necessary being the use of white margin cards.

Secretly note the bottom card and reverse it. Shuffle, leaving it there with one card below it. Fan the deck to show that the cards are well mixed, really your purpose is for your victim to note unconsciously that they all face one way. This is safe since the white margin only of the reversed card will show.

Tell a spectator that he seems to have all the characteristics of a successful magician and suggest that he try to do a trick. Hand the deck to him, show him how to spread the cards, thus avoiding any danger of his exposing the reversed card next the bottom. Draw a card and pretend to note what it is. Replace it and have him cut the pack once.

Say that to make a chosen card reverse itself amongst the rest all that is necessary is for him to "will" it to do so, the more strongly he concentrates his thoughts, the more likely he is to succeed, and so on. Finally name the card you reversed as being the card you just drew. Let him spread the cards face up. He finds one card face down. It is the card you named.

HILARIOUS FINISH TO AN OLD TRICK

From any pack a card is freely chosen by a spectator who is told to note it carefully without allowing any one to see what it is. The card is replaced, brought to the top and the pack shuffled, by whatever methods you prefer.

Announce that you will make the card appear at whatever number another spectator may call. Suppose eleven is chosen. Count off ten cards, taking the top one, the chosen card, first in the right hand, holding it with its outer end slanting downwards to avoid any exposure of its face, and putting the rest on it one by one. Let the spectator take the next card, the eleventh, off the deck face down. At once bring the right hand with the cards counted off, up to the pack, push the bottom card, the chosen one, to the left about an inch, and turn it face up at the moment the two packets are put together. The action takes but a moment and is covered by the back of the right hand.

The spectator says you have failed, the card is not his. Take it back and push it into the pack, anywhere above the reversed card. After a little argument suddenly perk up, remembering that the spectator should have held the pack himself. Give it to him to hold upright in his left hand, facing inwards. Tell him to count to the eleventh card, taking them off one by one slowly so that there will be no mistake, handing them to you as you stand beside him. When he has taken off the tenth card, stop him and take hold of his left wrist so that he must keep the pack in the same position, that is, with the reversed eleventh card facing the onlookers.

Ask him if he believes in telepathy. Say you are sure he will be an excellent transmitter and ask him to point out any one of the spectators to act as receiver. Remind him that no one but himself can possibly know what card he chose and impress on him that he must think intently of it and then ask the person to name it. The other spectator, entering into the joke, will call the name of the reversed card, much to the victim's bewilderment. After congratulating him on his great concentrative powers and so on, let him discover that his card is reversed.

This little comedy never fails to create amusement and really enhances the mystery as to how the chosen card arrived at the required number reversed.

SEEING IS BELIEVING

This feat depends on the intriguing principle of the introduction of a strange card into a borrowed deck. You have a card, say it is the Jack of Spades, from one of your own packs, face outwards, in your left trouser pocket. Borrow a deck and, under pretense of removing the Joker, or counting the cards to see if the deck is complete, sight the Jack of Spades, slip the left little finger tip below it and, in turning the pack face down, hold the break. Overhand shuffle to the break and throw the balance on top. This is the neatest way to get a required card to the top.

Offer the deck to a spectator to shuffle, palming the top card, the Jack of Spades, by the One Hand Palm (C. M. No. 1, p. 2). After a thorough shuffle let him place the pack on your left hand and make a free cut. Add the palmed card in taking up the remaining cards, put the cut below these, have the top card taken off and put in an envelope without being looked at. This method of forcing the Jack of Spades will be found quite convincing.

While the spectator is sealing and initialling the envelope, quietly palm your strange Jack of Spades in your left hand from trouser pocket and place the pack face up on it. Throw a handkerchief over the cards and invite a spectator to cut the pack thru the cover at any point he pleases. Turn the packet thus left on your left hand, bringing the Jack of Spades uppermost. Tell him to peek under the handkerchief and note the card at which he has cut, to take a good look at it and be sure to make no mistake. Let him drop the handkerchief, take the cut in your right hand and, still holding the packets separate under the cover, go to a second spectator and ask him to peek at the card in the same way. Do the same with a third person. Then again turn the lower packet and drop the cut on top. Turn the pack on its side and push up the left corner of the Jack of Spades. Grip this through the handkerchief and carry it away underneath in removing the handkerchief, which you crumple up and put in your pocket. You thus get rid of the strange card in a way that cannot possibly arouse any suspicion. Hand the deck to the spectator who holds the envelope.

Patter about cases of mistaken identity, how witnesses have been known to swear to having seen someone at a certain time, only to be proved mistaken, and so on. Ask the three spectators to name the card they have seen. They all name the Jack of Spades. Have the fourth spectator search the pack. There is no Jack of Spades in it. The others all assert positively that that is the card they all saw. Finally as proof positive that they have been mistaken, the envelope is opened and the Jack of Spades revealed.

As an impromptu feat, artfully led up to by turning the conversation to the subject of faulty observation and mistaken identity, this trick will be found wonderfully effective.

NOVEL BEGINNING FOR A FOUR ACE TRICK

Having secretly got the four aces to the bottom of the pack, riffle shuffle several times and make several false cuts, leaving the aces in position. Spread the deck and invite a spectator to touch any four cards at different points and to draw each card half way out without looking at the faces.

Close the fan, leaving the four cards protruding and secretly riffle off the four aces at the bottom with the right thumb, holding the break with the left little finger tip. Take the inner end of the pack, above the break, with the right thumb and middle finger and strip out the four protruding cards together with the four aces below them. At once drop the pack on the eight cards.

"Oh, my mistake," you exclaim, "I meant to put those four cards on the table." Draw off the four bottom cards, the aces, and put them face down on the table. Hand the pack to the spectator and, telling him you are going to show him a pretty trick with the aces, ask him to pick them out and at the same time to see that there are only four in the pack.

He fails to find any aces at all. The four cards on the table are turned over—they are the aces. Mr. Audley Walsh, the noted New Jersey magician, is the originator of this pretty feat.

THE NINES

Begin by handing a spectator a small pad and pencil and ask him to write a digit. Go to a second person and have him write one figure under the first. Do the same with a third, fourth and fifth spectator, possibly a sixth. You add the figures mentally as they are written and, when the total reaches thirty-seven or more, draw a line under the column, quickly adding one more figure to make the total forty-five. Hand the pad and pencil to still another spectator and have him add the figures, then add the two figures of the total. The result will be that one digit will have been arrived at, you say, by the purest chance. Let the person fold the paper and retain it without letting any one else see the final figure.

While this last operation was being done you have picked up a deck of cards and, quietly riffling it through, you have assembled the four nines on the top. Palm them in the right hand and offer the pack to be shuffled. This done have the pack put on your left hand and cut by the spectator. Pick up the lower packet, adding the palmed cards.

Deal the four nines face down on the table and have a spectator touch one. Place this card aside without showing its face. Reassemble the deck putting the three nines at the bottom.

Riffle count nine cards off the top under cover of squaring the deck with the right hand and hold a break at that point. Deal two or three cards rather quickly, then continue slowly, as you ask a spectator to call "Stop" whenever he pleases. You have to get just nine cards on the table, so if he calls before you reach the break, deal the last cards above it as one card. If, however, in spite of your dealing the last two or three cards very deliberately, he does not call until you have passed the break, put the extra cards a little over the side of the first nine so that you can easily palm off the unwanted cards in placing the packet aside. Get rid of the palmed cards at once by picking up the pack.

Spread the rest of the cards and have a spectator touch three and draw them half way out of the pack without looking at them. Close the spread and slip the tip of the little finger above the three bottom cards (nines), by riffling their inner ends with the right thumb. Grip the pack by the right thumb and middle finger at the inner end and, moving the left hand outwards carrying the three nines, strip out the protruding cards letting them fall on the nines. Drop the pack on top of the six cards and put it face down on the table.

The climax follows and is quite unexpected, since you have given no hint as to what is to follow. Patter about chance, fate, Kismet or what have you? Ask the spectator to unfold the slip and read the figure he arrived at ——————————— NINE.
Turn over the single card chosen ——————————— NINE.
Have the cards dealt out counted ——————————— NINE.
Turn the deck over and show the three ————————NINES.

THE FIVE CARD FAN

For an incomprehensible feat that practically works itself, this one is hard to beat. The effect is that five cards are shown to a spectator who notes one mentally. The five cards are partially inserted in the deck and a handkerchief is thrown over all. The spectator pushes these cards flush which causes several cards to protrude at the rear. These are pushed flush by the magician making some cards protrude at the front. Both repeat the movements until one card only extends from the outer end of the deck. The spectator takes it, still covered by the handkerchief and it proves to be the card thought of.

Arrange five cards in a fan and ask a spectator to remember one. You have the middle card fully exposed and you allow him to get a flash only of the cards so that he can only note that card. Then holding the deck face down in the left hand, open a break at the outer left corner, about the middle, with the left thumb. Insert the bottom card of the five, letting it protrude about three-quarters of its length. Riffle off one card with the left thumb and insert the next card in the same way. Do the same with the next three, saying that you are putting the cards in different parts of the pack and not letting it be seen that one card only is between each. Square the inner end of the deck and the outer ends of the five protruding cards.

Cover the cards with a handkerchief and instruct the spectator to push the cards flush with the deck. Doing so will force out four cards at the rear. You push these home forcing three cards to protrude from the outer end of the deck. Again the spectator pushes these into the deck, making two cards come out at the rear. You push these in and one card only emerges at the front. This will be the original middle card of the fan. Let the spectator take this card, through the handkerchief, as you draw the deck away. He names the card he thought of, removes the handkerchief and finds that very card in his hand.

NEW HALF PACK REVERSE

Having secretly reversed the bottom card, hold the pack face down in the left hand. Cut at about the center, opening the pack bookwise, the backs of the cards to the front. A moment before you separate your hands slide the bottom card of the right hand packet face up on top of the lower portion and at once turn the left hand over towards the right, showing this reversed card which will appear to be the bottom card of that packet. The move is covered by an upward motion of both hands as the cut is made.

Show both packets back and front. They appear to be perfectly regular and that in the right hand is, but the left hand packet has a card reversed both at the top and bottom. Turn this packet face up and and on it place the right hand packet face down, so that the packets overlap about half way. Hold them in this position vertically, right thumb at bottom and fingers on the top. The original reversed bottom card is towards the audience and the card reversed in the cut faces you. Show the packets back and front and it will appear that half faces downwards, the other half upwards.

If the two visible cards that face one another in the middle are of the same color you say that they should differ, or if they differ say that they should be alike; in either case, still holding the packets vertically, slide out the faced card of the lower packet, turn it over and insert it in the top packet. "That's better," you say, and at once push the two packets together, square the deck and hold it face down.

Pull out the bottom card and with it fan the deck, then drop it face down on top. Spread the cards out on the table with a flourish. All of them face the same way.

THE DANISH FORCE

This is a comedy force originated by Clement de Lion. The idea is to have a card push itself forward spontaneously just as the spectator is about to take a card. De Lion used the old fake, two cards with a piece of elastic between them. The card to be forced was pushed into the fake and so held. The pressure being relaxed as the spectator reached out, the card would glide into his hand.

It is, however, a difficult matter to insert the fake in the pack and prevent the card making premature appearance. A simpler plan is to use the even older principle of the rising card. Take a length of fine black silk, about eighteen inches, tie a knot at one end and insert it in a minute slit in the end of the card to be used. Draw the thread over the back of this card, place a second card on it and bring the thread back over it. To the other end of the thread tie a small black safety pin, fastening it under the vest.

If these two cards are placed in the pack, when it is thrust outwards, the card will glide out to meet the spectator's hand. As he takes it, the withdrawal of the pack will free the thread. The two cards thus prepared can be carried quite safely in the lower vest pocket. To add them to the deck is an easy matter and a simple cut will bring them to the middle.

This amusing feat makes a very good opening for the Ambitious Card trick. Say you use the Jack of Diamonds. After the comedy force inquire what the card is. "The Jack of Diamonds," you say. "That's the most troublesome card in the deck. Always pushing himself forward. Put him on the top out of the way and take another." You pass the card to the middle and again force it by the classical method. Then continue with your own favorite version of the Ambitious Card, that always returns to the top of the pack.

YOUR CARD, SIR?

This trick was contributed by me to the Sphinx for July, 1936, and is reproduced by permission. It is an elaboration of a somewhat old experiment. The requirements are: a small table, a pack of cards and a plain sheet of glass about six by four inches in size. Begin by inviting a spectator to help you and ask him to bring his hat with him. Seat the gentleman on your left, take his hat and put it crown downwards on the table, taking the opportunity to press the sweat band open a little on one side. Hand the cards to the gentleman, let him shuffle it to his own satisfaction, retain one card and return the rest to you.

The next step is to have the card returned to the deck, brought to the top, and, if desired, palmed off and the deck again shuffled. The method I leave to the individual performer, suggesting, however, that the use of the Hindu shuffle is as good as any. Take the pack replacing the palmed card on top, and have the assistant cut it into two parts, as nearly equal as possible. Let him touch one packet. If he touches that with the chosen card on the top say, "I am to use this one? Very well," and take it. On the other hand if he touches the other packet say, "You wish to have that one? Take it, please." Continue, "Now I want you to do exactly as I do." With that take your packet and rip it in half. Put one half down and tear the remainder in half again. Place these two quarter packets face down on the table and pick up the other half packet. Tear this in half and place the resulting quarter packets beside the other two. While you are doing this the assistant will probably be still struggling with his half. However, take no notice. Go right on.

Pick up the quarter packet that looks the smallest. With the back of your hand to the audience, dribble out the pieces in a stream into the hat. At the same time pull back the top piece into the finger palm position with your thumb. Take up the next largest packet and repeat the operation. Continue with the remaining packets, keeping the largest to the last, since this will aid you in holding the other three pieces easily and cleanly. Dip your hand into the hat and stir the pieces around, taking the opportunity to slip the four pieces of the chosen card under the sweat band at the point where you had previously pulled it open, so making the operation an easy one.

Now grasp the hat with the fingers inside covering the position of the four pieces and holding them securely, and turn your attention to your volunteer assistant. Probably he has not succeeded in tearing his cards in half even, but in any case let him finish quartering his cards over the hat so that the audience see the pieces drop in with the others. At this point it is advisable to recapitulate what has been done — a card has been chosen, the deck shuffled and the pack torn to fragments. Introduce the sheet of glass, on one side of which you have previously placed four tiny pellets of wax, so that they form the corners of a square in the center of the glass about one and a half inches apart. Hand it to your assistant and have him hold it in full view, waxed side uppermost. Touch his hand with your finger tips under the excuse of getting the vibrations of the chosen card. Show your hand empty, dip it into the hat, stir the pieces around and draw out one piece from under the band. Hold it with its back to the audience and press it face down on one of the pellets of wax on the glass. This operation you repeat three times, but for the last piece let the assistant stir the pieces in the hat himself, then touch his hand again and bring out the last piece.

The fragments of course, have been placed in their proper positions on the pellets of wax so that when you have the gentleman call the name of his card it is only necessary for him to hold up the glass towards the audience and everyone sees at once that you have restored the chosen card, its face showing plainly through the glass.

This method of revealing the card at the finish is new and may be used to good advantage in other tricks. For a whole card one pellet of wax only will suffice.

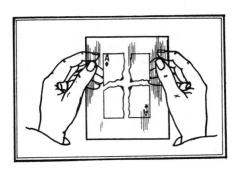

Part IV.—The Palm and Recovery

This very effective flourish deserves much better treatment than it usually receives, even at the hands of professional magicians. How often does one see the artist palpably grab a handful of cards from the top of the pack, then thrust his hand under the coat of a spectator and bring them out spread fanwise? The spectators laugh and applaud and the performer takes it all as the reward of his cleverness. In reality the spectators have seen exactly what he really did, there was no secret in his getting possession of the cards, and they only laughed at the discomfiture of the volunteer assistant. Having "got away with it" so easily, as he thinks, he never sees any necessity for making his moves cleanly. Yet the palm and recovery should be done in such a way that it creates real mystery as well as amusement.

In the first place when you palm the cards never remove the right hand at once. Hold the pack in the same hand for a few moments and then transfer it to the left hand as openly as possible. Close the second, third and fourth fingers, bending the cards almost double, and with the forefinger point to the place from which you are about to produce the cards. Thrust your hand under the spectator's coat and rest it momentarily flat against his body. Bend your middle finger inward, pressing its tip on the back of the packet to hold it as you withdraw your hand a little to enable you to grip the inner ends of the cards by the finger tips. Then fan the cards to the fullest possible extent as you bring them into view. The whole action should be made as if your hand went to the spectator's coat to take out cards you just pointed to and not to push them underneath it. In this way you get not only the amusement of the onlookers but their mystification as well.

When the cards are to be produced from the performer's body, the action differs. Suppose the fan of cards is to be produced from the back of your right knee, palm the packet and retain the pack in the right hand as you make a free gesture with the left. Then take the pack in that hand as openly as possible and make a one hand color change, pointing to the face card with the right forefinger, the other three fingers bending the cards into the palm. Ruffle the pack, look down at your knee and drop your right hand just behind it. Insert the first joint of your middle finger behind the packet and, by straightening the fingers, extend the cards directly behind your knee. Grip the cloth of your trouser leg with the tips of your thumb and middle finger and pull it outwards, palm of the hand to the front, tips of the fingers and the cards behind the cloth. Fan the cards as you draw them into view and it will appear as if they are being actually pulled through the fabric.

If the palmed cards are to be apparently caught in mid-air, then, as you stretch your arm out, grip them by their outer ends between the tips of the first and second fingers at one corner and between the third and fourth fingers at the other, exactly as in the front palm for the back and front sleight. Bend the thumb in on the back of the cards and fan them out as widely as possible. By varying the methods of making the palm and the single hand color change, a routine of moves can be arranged which will be really mystifying and not mere jugglery. The Hugard palm will be found a valuable one for this purpose since the bottom card remains in full view, making it appear to be impossible that any cards could have been palmed off. The flourish given on p. 71, C. M. No. 3, will also be found to fit into such a routine with very good effect.

FINALE

At the conclusion of a series of card tricks the magician scales out a few cards to the spectators and then throws the whole deck, this bursts open in mid-air and a shower of colored tissue butterflies flutter down on the audience with beautiful effect.

Make up a packet of tissue butterflies, of bright colors, about the size of the cards. Paste a band of tissue round the packet with a loop of fine wire passing round the band on the lower side. Attach a length of black silk to the wire loop and on the packet put six or eight loose cards of the same pattern as the pack in use. Set the packet on your table, carry the silk over the front edge and coil it carefully on the floor under the table, tieing the loose end to the table leg. If the packet is thrown out forcibly, on reaching the limit of the silk, the wire loop will cut the tissue band, the butterflies will be released and flutter down on the spectators.

To make the necessary change of the deck for the prepared packet, cover the latter with a handkerchief. Pick this up with your left hand and apparently put the pack down, really palming it as you put your hand on the packet. Delicately wipe your finger tips, then thrust the handkerchief and the palmed cards in your pocket. Pick up the prepared packet and scale out the loose cards on top, then throw out the packet. Toss it high up so that the wire loop and silk will recoil on the stage where they will lie unnoticed.

Buatier de Kolta used round discs of tissue with his name on them. His thread was fastened to the back of the stage and, after the throw his assistant would rapidly gather it in.

THE END

A CATALOG OF SELECTED

DOVER BOOKS

IN ALL FIELDS OF INTEREST

A CATALOG OF SELECTED DOVER
BOOKS IN ALL FIELDS OF INTEREST

CONCERNING THE SPIRITUAL IN ART, Wassily Kandinsky. Pioneering work by father of abstract art. Thoughts on color theory, nature of art. Analysis of earlier masters. 12 illustrations. 80pp. of text. 5⅜ x 8½.   23411-8 Pa. $4.95

ANIMALS: 1,419 Copyright-Free Illustrations of Mammals, Birds, Fish, Insects, etc., Jim Harter (ed.). Clear wood engravings present, in extremely lifelike poses, over 1,000 species of animals. One of the most extensive pictorial sourcebooks of its kind. Captions. Index. 284pp. 9 x 12.   23766-4 Pa. $14.95

CELTIC ART: The Methods of Construction, George Bain. Simple geometric techniques for making Celtic interlacements, spirals, Kells-type initials, animals, humans, etc. Over 500 illustrations. 160pp. 9 x 12. (USO)   22923-8 Pa. $9.95

AN ATLAS OF ANATOMY FOR ARTISTS, Fritz Schider. Most thorough reference work on art anatomy in the world. Hundreds of illustrations, including selections from works by Vesalius, Leonardo, Goya, Ingres, Michelangelo, others. 593 illustrations. 192pp. 7⅛ x 10¼.   20241-0 Pa. $9.95

CELTIC HAND STROKE-BY-STROKE (Irish Half-Uncial from "The Book of Kells"): An Arthur Baker Calligraphy Manual, Arthur Baker. Complete guide to creating each letter of the alphabet in distinctive Celtic manner. Covers hand position, strokes, pens, inks, paper, more. Illustrated. 48pp. 8¼ x 11.   24336-2 Pa. $3.95

EASY ORIGAMI, John Montroll. Charming collection of 32 projects (hat, cup, pelican, piano, swan, many more) specially designed for the novice origami hobbyist. Clearly illustrated easy-to-follow instructions insure that even beginning papercrafters will achieve successful results. 48pp. 8¼ x 11.   27298-2 Pa. $3.50

THE COMPLETE BOOK OF BIRDHOUSE CONSTRUCTION FOR WOOD-WORKERS, Scott D. Campbell. Detailed instructions, illustrations, tables. Also data on bird habitat and instinct patterns. Bibliography. 3 tables. 63 illustrations in 15 figures. 48pp. 5¼ x 8½.   24407-5 Pa. $2.50

BLOOMINGDALE'S ILLUSTRATED 1886 CATALOG: Fashions, Dry Goods and Housewares, Bloomingdale Brothers. Famed merchants' extremely rare catalog depicting about 1,700 products: clothing, housewares, firearms, dry goods, jewelry, more. Invaluable for dating, identifying vintage items. Also, copyright-free graphics for artists, designers. Co-published with Henry Ford Museum & Greenfield Village. 160pp. 8¼ x 11.   25780-0 Pa. $10.95

HISTORIC COSTUME IN PICTURES, Braun & Schneider. Over 1,450 costumed figures in clearly detailed engravings–from dawn of civilization to end of 19th century. Captions. Many folk costumes. 256pp. 8⅜ x 11¾.   23150-X Pa. $12.95

STICKLEY CRAFTSMAN FURNITURE CATALOGS, Gustav Stickley and L. & J. G. Stickley. Beautiful, functional furniture in two authentic catalogs from 1910. 594 illustrations, including 277 photos, show settles, rockers, armchairs, reclining chairs, bookcases, desks, tables. 183pp. 6½ x 9¼. 23838-5 Pa. $11.95

AMERICAN LOCOMOTIVES IN HISTORIC PHOTOGRAPHS: 1858 to 1949, Ron Ziel (ed.). A rare collection of 126 meticulously detailed official photographs, called "builder portraits," of American locomotives that majestically chronicle the rise of steam locomotive power in America. Introduction. Detailed captions. xi + 129pp. 9 x 12. 27393-8 Pa. $13.95

AMERICA'S LIGHTHOUSES: An Illustrated History, Francis Ross Holland, Jr. Delightfully written, profusely illustrated fact-filled survey of over 200 American lighthouses since 1716. History, anecdotes, technological advances, more. 240pp. 8 x 10¾. 25576-X Pa. $12.95

TOWARDS A NEW ARCHITECTURE, Le Corbusier. Pioneering manifesto by founder of "International School." Technical and aesthetic theories, views of industry, economics, relation of form to function, "mass-production split" and much more. Profusely illustrated. 320pp. 6⅛ x 9¼. (USO) 25023-7 Pa. $9.95

HOW THE OTHER HALF LIVES, Jacob Riis. Famous journalistic record, exposing poverty and degradation of New York slums around 1900, by major social reformer. 100 striking and influential photographs. 233pp. 10 x 7⅞. 22012-5 Pa. $11.95

FRUIT KEY AND TWIG KEY TO TREES AND SHRUBS, William M. Harlow. One of the handiest and most widely used identification aids. Fruit key covers 120 deciduous and evergreen species; twig key 160 deciduous species. Easily used. Over 300 photographs. 126pp. 5⅜ x 8½. 20511-8 Pa. $3.95

COMMON BIRD SONGS, Dr. Donald J. Borror. Songs of 60 most common U.S. birds: robins, sparrows, cardinals, bluejays, finches, more–arranged in order of increasing complexity. Up to 9 variations of songs of each species. Cassette and manual 99911-4 $8.95

ORCHIDS AS HOUSE PLANTS, Rebecca Tyson Northen. Grow cattleyas and many other kinds of orchids–in a window, in a case, or under artificial light. 63 illustrations. 148pp. 5⅜ x 8½. 23261-1 Pa. $5.95

MONSTER MAZES, Dave Phillips. Masterful mazes at four levels of difficulty. Avoid deadly perils and evil creatures to find magical treasures. Solutions for all 32 exciting illustrated puzzles. 48pp. 8¼ x 11. 26005-4 Pa. $2.95

MOZART'S DON GIOVANNI (DOVER OPERA LIBRETTO SERIES), Wolfgang Amadeus Mozart. Introduced and translated by Ellen H. Bleiler. Standard Italian libretto, with complete English translation. Convenient and thoroughly portable–an ideal companion for reading along with a recording or the performance itself. Introduction. List of characters. Plot summary. 121pp. 5¼ x 8½. 24944-1 Pa. $3.95

TECHNICAL MANUAL AND DICTIONARY OF CLASSICAL BALLET, Gail Grant. Defines, explains, comments on steps, movements, poses and concepts. 15-page pictorial section. Basic book for student, viewer. 127pp. 5⅜ x 8½. 21843-0 Pa. $4.95

BRASS INSTRUMENTS: Their History and Development, Anthony Baines. Authoritative, updated survey of the evolution of trumpets, trombones, bugles, cornets, French horns, tubas and other brass wind instruments. Over 140 illustrations and 48 music examples. Corrected and updated by author. New preface. Bibliography. 320pp. 5⅜ x 8½. 27574-4 Pa. $9.95

HOLLYWOOD GLAMOR PORTRAITS, John Kobal (ed.). 145 photos from 1926-49. Harlow, Gable, Bogart, Bacall; 94 stars in all. Full background on photographers, technical aspects. 160pp. 8⅜ x 11¼. 23352-9 Pa. $12.95

MAX AND MORITZ, Wilhelm Busch. Great humor classic in both German and English. Also 10 other works: "Cat and Mouse," "Plisch and Plumm," etc. 216pp. 5⅜ x 8½. 20181-3 Pa. $6.95

THE RAVEN AND OTHER FAVORITE POEMS, Edgar Allan Poe. Over 40 of the author's most memorable poems: "The Bells," "Ulalume," "Israfel," "To Helen," "The Conqueror Worm," "Eldorado," "Annabel Lee," many more. Alphabetic lists of titles and first lines. 64pp. 5 3/16 x 8¼. 26685-0 Pa. $1.00

PERSONAL MEMOIRS OF U. S. GRANT, Ulysses Simpson Grant. Intelligent, deeply moving firsthand account of Civil War campaigns, considered by many the finest military memoirs ever written. Includes letters, historic photographs, maps and more. 528pp. 6⅛ x 9¼. 28587-1 Pa. $12.95

AMULETS AND SUPERSTITIONS, E. A. Wallis Budge. Comprehensive discourse on origin, powers of amulets in many ancient cultures: Arab, Persian Babylonian, Assyrian, Egyptian, Gnostic, Hebrew, Phoenician, Syriac, etc. Covers cross, swastika, crucifix, seals, rings, stones, etc. 584pp. 5⅜ x 8½. 23573-4 Pa. $15.95

RUSSIAN STORIES/PYCCKNE PACCKA3bl: A Dual-Language Book, edited by Gleb Struve. Twelve tales by such masters as Chekhov, Tolstoy, Dostoevsky, Pushkin, others. Excellent word-for-word English translations on facing pages, plus teaching and study aids, Russian/English vocabulary, biographical/critical introductions, more. 416pp. 5⅜ x 8½. 26244-8 Pa. $9.95

PHILADELPHIA THEN AND NOW: 60 Sites Photographed in the Past and Present, Kenneth Finkel and Susan Oyama. Rare photographs of City Hall, Logan Square, Independence Hall, Betsy Ross House, other landmarks juxtaposed with contemporary views. Captures changing face of historic city. Introduction. Captions. 128pp. 8¼ x 11. 25790-8 Pa. $9.95

AIA ARCHITECTURAL GUIDE TO NASSAU AND SUFFOLK COUNTIES, LONG ISLAND, The American Institute of Architects, Long Island Chapter, and the Society for the Preservation of Long Island Antiquities. Comprehensive, well-researched and generously illustrated volume brings to life over three centuries of Long Island's great architectural heritage. More than 240 photographs with authoritative, extensively detailed captions. 176pp. 8¼ x 11. 26946-9 Pa. $14.95

NORTH AMERICAN INDIAN LIFE: Customs and Traditions of 23 Tribes, Elsie Clews Parsons (ed.). 27 fictionalized essays by noted anthropologists examine religion, customs, government, additional facets of life among the Winnebago, Crow, Zuni, Eskimo, other tribes. 480pp. 6⅛ x 9¼. 27377-6 Pa. $10.95

FRANK LLOYD WRIGHT'S HOLLYHOCK HOUSE, Donald Hoffmann. Lavishly illustrated, carefully documented study of one of Wright's most controversial residential designs. Over 120 photographs, floor plans, elevations, etc. Detailed perceptive text by noted Wright scholar. Index. 128pp. 9¼ x 10¾. 27133-1 Pa. $11.95

THE MALE AND FEMALE FIGURE IN MOTION: 60 Classic Photographic Sequences, Eadweard Muybridge. 60 true-action photographs of men and women walking, running, climbing, bending, turning, etc., reproduced from rare 19th-century masterpiece. vi + 121pp. 9 x 12. 24745-7 Pa. $10.95

1001 QUESTIONS ANSWERED ABOUT THE SEASHORE, N. J. Berrill and Jacquelyn Berrill. Queries answered about dolphins, sea snails, sponges, starfish, fishes, shore birds, many others. Covers appearance, breeding, growth, feeding, much more. 305pp. 5¼ x 8¼. 23366-9 Pa. $9.95

GUIDE TO OWL WATCHING IN NORTH AMERICA, Donald S. Heintzelman. Superb guide offers complete data and descriptions of 19 species: barn owl, screech owl, snowy owl, many more. Expert coverage of owl-watching equipment, conservation, migrations and invasions, etc. Guide to observing sites. 84 illustrations. xiii + 193pp. 5⅜ x 8½. 27344-X Pa. $8.95

MEDICINAL AND OTHER USES OF NORTH AMERICAN PLANTS: A Historical Survey with Special Reference to the Eastern Indian Tribes, Charlotte Erichsen-Brown. Chronological historical citations document 500 years of usage of plants, trees, shrubs native to eastern Canada, northeastern U.S. Also complete identifying information. 343 illustrations. 544pp. 6½ x 9¼. 25951-X Pa. $12.95

STORYBOOK MAZES, Dave Phillips. 23 stories and mazes on two-page spreads: Wizard of Oz, Treasure Island, Robin Hood, etc. Solutions. 64pp. 8¼ x 11. 23628-5 Pa. $2.95

NEGRO FOLK MUSIC, U.S.A., Harold Courlander. Noted folklorist's scholarly yet readable analysis of rich and varied musical tradition. Includes authentic versions of over 40 folk songs. Valuable bibliography and discography. xi + 324pp. 5⅜ x 8½. 27350-4 Pa. $9.95

MOVIE-STAR PORTRAITS OF THE FORTIES, John Kobal (ed.). 163 glamor, studio photos of 106 stars of the 1940s: Rita Hayworth, Ava Gardner, Marlon Brando, Clark Gable, many more. 176pp. 8⅜ x 11¼. 23546-7 Pa. $14.95

BENCHLEY LOST AND FOUND, Robert Benchley. Finest humor from early 30s, about pet peeves, child psychologists, post office and others. Mostly unavailable elsewhere. 73 illustrations by Peter Arno and others. 183pp. 5⅜ x 8½. 22410-4 Pa. $6.95

YEKL and THE IMPORTED BRIDEGROOM AND OTHER STORIES OF YIDDISH NEW YORK, Abraham Cahan. Film Hester Street based on Yekl (1896). Novel, other stories among first about Jewish immigrants on N.Y.'s East Side. 240pp. 5⅜ x 8½. 22427-9 Pa. $6.95

SELECTED POEMS, Walt Whitman. Generous sampling from *Leaves of Grass*. Twenty-four poems include "I Hear America Singing," "Song of the Open Road," "I Sing the Body Electric," "When Lilacs Last in the Dooryard Bloom'd," "O Captain! My Captain!"—all reprinted from an authoritative edition. Lists of titles and first lines. 128pp. 5³⁄₁₆ x 8¼. 26878-0 Pa. $1.00

THE BEST TALES OF HOFFMANN, E. T. A. Hoffmann. 10 of Hoffmann's most important stories: "Nutcracker and the King of Mice," "The Golden Flowerpot," etc. 458pp. 5⅜ x 8½. 21793-0 Pa. $9.95

FROM FETISH TO GOD IN ANCIENT EGYPT, E. A. Wallis Budge. Rich detailed survey of Egyptian conception of "God" and gods, magic, cult of animals, Osiris, more. Also, superb English translations of hymns and legends. 240 illustrations. 545pp. 5⅜ x 8½. 25803-3 Pa. $13.95

FRENCH STORIES/CONTES FRANÇAIS: A Dual-Language Book, Wallace Fowlie. Ten stories by French masters, Voltaire to Camus: "Micromegas" by Voltaire; "The Atheist's Mass" by Balzac; "Minuet" by de Maupassant; "The Guest" by Camus, six more. Excellent English translations on facing pages. Also French-English vocabulary list, exercises, more. 352pp. 5⅜ x 8½. 26443-2 Pa. $9.95

CHICAGO AT THE TURN OF THE CENTURY IN PHOTOGRAPHS: 122 Historic Views from the Collections of the Chicago Historical Society, Larry A. Viskochil. Rare large-format prints offer detailed views of City Hall, State Street, the Loop, Hull House, Union Station, many other landmarks, circa 1904-1913. Introduction. Captions. Maps. 144pp. 9⅜ x 12¼. 24656-6 Pa. $12.95

OLD BROOKLYN IN EARLY PHOTOGRAPHS, 1865-1929, William Lee Younger. Luna Park, Gravesend race track, construction of Grand Army Plaza, moving of Hotel Brighton, etc. 157 previously unpublished photographs. 165pp. 8⅞ x 11¾. 23587-4 Pa. $13.95

THE MYTHS OF THE NORTH AMERICAN INDIANS, Lewis Spence. Rich anthology of the myths and legends of the Algonquins, Iroquois, Pawnees and Sioux, prefaced by an extensive historical and ethnological commentary. 36 illustrations. 480pp. 5⅜ x 8½. 25967-6 Pa. $10.95

AN ENCYCLOPEDIA OF BATTLES: Accounts of Over 1,560 Battles from 1479 B.C. to the Present, David Eggenberger. Essential details of every major battle in recorded history from the first battle of Megiddo in 1479 B.C. to Grenada in 1984. List of Battle Maps. New Appendix covering the years 1967-1984. Index. 99 illustrations. 544pp. 6½ x 9¼. 24913-1 Pa. $16.95

SAILING ALONE AROUND THE WORLD, Captain Joshua Slocum. First man to sail around the world, alone, in small boat. One of great feats of seamanship told in delightful manner. 67 illustrations. 294pp. 5⅜ x 8½. 20326-3 Pa. $6.95

ANARCHISM AND OTHER ESSAYS, Emma Goldman. Powerful, penetrating, prophetic essays on direct action, role of minorities, prison reform, puritan hypocrisy, violence, etc. 271pp. 5⅜ x 8½. 22484-8 Pa. $7.95

MYTHS OF THE HINDUS AND BUDDHISTS, Ananda K. Coomaraswamy and Sister Nivedita. Great stories of the epics; deeds of Krishna, Shiva, taken from puranas, Vedas, folk tales; etc. 32 illustrations. 400pp. 5⅜ x 8½. 21759-0 Pa. $12.95

BEYOND PSYCHOLOGY, Otto Rank. Fear of death, desire of immortality, nature of sexuality, social organization, creativity, according to Rankian system. 291pp. 5⅜ x 8½. 20485-5 Pa. $8.95

A THEOLOGICO-POLITICAL TREATISE, Benedict Spinoza. Also contains unfinished Political Treatise. Great classic on religious liberty, theory of government on common consent. R. Elwes translation. Total of 421pp. 5⅜ x 8½. 20249-6 Pa. $9.95

MY BONDAGE AND MY FREEDOM, Frederick Douglass. Born a slave, Douglass became outspoken force in antislavery movement. The best of Douglass' autobiographies. Graphic description of slave life. 464pp. 5⅜ x 8½. 22457-0 Pa. $8.95

FOLLOWING THE EQUATOR: A Journey Around the World, Mark Twain. Fascinating humorous account of 1897 voyage to Hawaii, Australia, India, New Zealand, etc. Ironic, bemused reports on peoples, customs, climate, flora and fauna, politics, much more. 197 illustrations. 720pp. 5⅜ x 8½. 26113-1 Pa. $15.95

THE PEOPLE CALLED SHAKERS, Edward D. Andrews. Definitive study of Shakers: origins, beliefs, practices, dances, social organization, furniture and crafts, etc. 33 illustrations. 351pp. 5⅜ x 8½. 21081-2 Pa. $8.95

THE MYTHS OF GREECE AND ROME, H. A. Guerber. A classic of mythology, generously illustrated, long prized for its simple, graphic, accurate retelling of the principal myths of Greece and Rome, and for its commentary on their origins and significance. With 64 illustrations by Michelangelo, Raphael, Titian, Rubens, Canova, Bernini and others. 480pp. 5⅜ x 8½. 27584-1 Pa. $9.95

PSYCHOLOGY OF MUSIC, Carl E. Seashore. Classic work discusses music as a medium from psychological viewpoint. Clear treatment of physical acoustics, auditory apparatus, sound perception, development of musical skills, nature of musical feeling, host of other topics. 88 figures. 408pp. 5⅜ x 8½. 21851-1 Pa. $11.95

THE PHILOSOPHY OF HISTORY, Georg W. Hegel. Great classic of Western thought develops concept that history is not chance but rational process, the evolution of freedom. 457pp. 5⅜ x 8½. 20112-0 Pa. $9.95

THE BOOK OF TEA, Kakuzo Okakura. Minor classic of the Orient: entertaining, charming explanation, interpretation of traditional Japanese culture in terms of tea ceremony. 94pp. 5⅜ x 8½. 20070-1 Pa. $3.95

LIFE IN ANCIENT EGYPT, Adolf Erman. Fullest, most thorough, detailed older account with much not in more recent books, domestic life, religion, magic, medicine, commerce, much more. Many illustrations reproduce tomb paintings, carvings, hieroglyphs, etc. 597pp. 5⅜ x 8½. 22632-8 Pa. $12.95

SUNDIALS, Their Theory and Construction, Albert Waugh. Far and away the best, most thorough coverage of ideas, mathematics concerned, types, construction, adjusting anywhere. Simple, nontechnical treatment allows even children to build several of these dials. Over 100 illustrations. 230pp. 5⅜ x 8½. 22947-5 Pa. $8.95

DYNAMICS OF FLUIDS IN POROUS MEDIA, Jacob Bear. For advanced students of ground water hydrology, soil mechanics and physics, drainage and irrigation engineering, and more. 335 illustrations. Exercises, with answers. 784pp. 6⅛ x 9¼. 65675-6 Pa. $19.95

SONGS OF EXPERIENCE: Facsimile Reproduction with 26 Plates in Full Color, William Blake. 26 full-color plates from a rare 1826 edition. Includes "The Tyger," "London," "Holy Thursday," and other poems. Printed text of poems. 48pp. 5¼ x 7. 24636-1 Pa. $4.95

OLD-TIME VIGNETTES IN FULL COLOR, Carol Belanger Grafton (ed.). Over 390 charming, often sentimental illustrations, selected from archives of Victorian graphics–pretty women posing, children playing, food, flowers, kittens and puppies, smiling cherubs, birds and butterflies, much more. All copyright-free. 48pp. 9¼ x 12¼. 27269-9 Pa. $7.95

PERSPECTIVE FOR ARTISTS, Rex Vicat Cole. Depth, perspective of sky and sea, shadows, much more, not usually covered. 391 diagrams, 81 reproductions of drawings and paintings. 279pp. 5⅜ x 8½. 22487-2 Pa. $7.95

DRAWING THE LIVING FIGURE, Joseph Sheppard. Innovative approach to artistic anatomy focuses on specifics of surface anatomy, rather than muscles and bones. Over 170 drawings of live models in front, back and side views, and in widely varying poses. Accompanying diagrams. 177 illustrations. Introduction. Index. 144pp. 8⅜ x11¼. 26723-7 Pa. $8.95

GOTHIC AND OLD ENGLISH ALPHABETS: 100 Complete Fonts, Dan X. Solo. Add power, elegance to posters, signs, other graphics with 100 stunning copyright-free alphabets: Blackstone, Dolbey, Germania, 97 more–including many lower-case, numerals, punctuation marks. 104pp. 8⅛ x 11. 24695-7 Pa. $8.95

HOW TO DO BEADWORK, Mary White. Fundamental book on craft from simple projects to five-bead chains and woven works. 106 illustrations. 142pp. 5⅜ x 8. 20697-1 Pa. $5.95

THE BOOK OF WOOD CARVING, Charles Marshall Sayers. Finest book for beginners discusses fundamentals and offers 34 designs. "Absolutely first rate . . . well thought out and well executed."–E. J. Tangerman. 118pp. 7¾ x 10⅝. 23654-4 Pa. $7.95

ILLUSTRATED CATALOG OF CIVIL WAR MILITARY GOODS: Union Army Weapons, Insignia, Uniform Accessories, and Other Equipment, Schuyler, Hartley, and Graham. Rare, profusely illustrated 1846 catalog includes Union Army uniform and dress regulations, arms and ammunition, coats, insignia, flags, swords, rifles, etc. 226 illustrations. 160pp. 9 x 12. 24939-5 Pa. $10.95

WOMEN'S FASHIONS OF THE EARLY 1900s: An Unabridged Republication of "New York Fashions, 1909," National Cloak & Suit Co. Rare catalog of mail-order fashions documents women's and children's clothing styles shortly after the turn of the century. Captions offer full descriptions, prices. Invaluable resource for fashion, costume historians. Approximately 725 illustrations. 128pp. 8⅜ x 11¼. 27276-1 Pa. $11.95

THE 1912 AND 1915 GUSTAV STICKLEY FURNITURE CATALOGS, Gustav Stickley. With over 200 detailed illustrations and descriptions, these two catalogs are essential reading and reference materials and identification guides for Stickley furniture. Captions cite materials, dimensions and prices. 112pp. 6½ x 9¼. 26676-1 Pa. $9.95

EARLY AMERICAN LOCOMOTIVES, John H. White, Jr. Finest locomotive engravings from early 19th century: historical (1804–74), main-line (after 1870), special, foreign, etc. 147 plates. 142pp. 11⅜ x 8¼. 22772-3 Pa. $10.95

THE TALL SHIPS OF TODAY IN PHOTOGRAPHS, Frank O. Braynard. Lavishly illustrated tribute to nearly 100 majestic contemporary sailing vessels: Amerigo Vespucci, Clearwater, Constitution, Eagle, Mayflower, Sea Cloud, Victory, many more. Authoritative captions provide statistics, background on each ship. 190 black-and-white photographs and illustrations. Introduction. 128pp. 8⅞ x 11¾. 27163-3 Pa. $14.95

EARLY NINETEENTH-CENTURY CRAFTS AND TRADES, Peter Stockham (ed.). Extremely rare 1807 volume describes to youngsters the crafts and trades of the day: brickmaker, weaver, dressmaker, bookbinder, ropemaker, saddler, many more. Quaint prose, charming illustrations for each craft. 20 black-and-white line illustrations. 192pp. 4⅝ x 6. 27293-1 Pa. $4.95

VICTORIAN FASHIONS AND COSTUMES FROM HARPER'S BAZAR, 1867–1898, Stella Blum (ed.). Day costumes, evening wear, sports clothes, shoes, hats, other accessories in over 1,000 detailed engravings. 320pp. 9⅜ x 12¼. 22990-4 Pa. $15.95

GUSTAV STICKLEY, THE CRAFTSMAN, Mary Ann Smith. Superb study surveys broad scope of Stickley's achievement, especially in architecture. Design philosophy, rise and fall of the Craftsman empire, descriptions and floor plans for many Craftsman houses, more. 86 black-and-white halftones. 31 line illustrations. Introduction 208pp. 6½ x 9¼. 27210-9 Pa. $9.95

THE LONG ISLAND RAIL ROAD IN EARLY PHOTOGRAPHS, Ron Ziel. Over 220 rare photos, informative text document origin (1844) and development of rail service on Long Island. Vintage views of early trains, locomotives, stations, passengers, crews, much more. Captions. 8⅞ x 11¾. 26301-0 Pa. $13.95

THE BOOK OF OLD SHIPS: From Egyptian Galleys to Clipper Ships, Henry B. Culver. Superb, authoritative history of sailing vessels, with 80 magnificent line illustrations. Galley, bark, caravel, longship, whaler, many more. Detailed, informative text on each vessel by noted naval historian. Introduction. 256pp. 5⅜ x 8½. 27332-6 Pa. $7.95

TEN BOOKS ON ARCHITECTURE, Vitruvius. The most important book ever written on architecture. Early Roman aesthetics, technology, classical orders, site selection, all other aspects. Morgan translation. 331pp. 5⅜ x 8½. 20645-9 Pa. $8.95

THE HUMAN FIGURE IN MOTION, Eadweard Muybridge. More than 4,500 stopped-action photos, in action series, showing undraped men, women, children jumping, lying down, throwing, sitting, wrestling, carrying, etc. 390pp. 7⅞ x 10⅝. 20204-6 Clothbd. $27.95

TREES OF THE EASTERN AND CENTRAL UNITED STATES AND CANADA, William M. Harlow. Best one-volume guide to 140 trees. Full descriptions, woodlore, range, etc. Over 600 illustrations. Handy size. 288pp. 4½ x 6⅜. 20395-6 Pa. $6.95

SONGS OF WESTERN BIRDS, Dr. Donald J. Borror. Complete song and call repertoire of 60 western species, including flycatchers, juncoes, cactus wrens, many more–includes fully illustrated booklet. Cassette and manual 99913-0 $8.95

GROWING AND USING HERBS AND SPICES, Milo Miloradovich. Versatile handbook provides all the information needed for cultivation and use of all the herbs and spices available in North America. 4 illustrations. Index. Glossary. 236pp. 5⅜ x 8½. 25058-X Pa. $7.95

BIG BOOK OF MAZES AND LABYRINTHS, Walter Shepherd. 50 mazes and labyrinths in all–classical, solid, ripple, and more–in one great volume. Perfect inexpensive puzzler for clever youngsters. Full solutions. 112pp. 8⅛ x 11. 22951-3 Pa. $4.95

PIANO TUNING, J. Cree Fischer. Clearest, best book for beginner, amateur. Simple repairs, raising dropped notes, tuning by easy method of flattened fifths. No previous skills needed. 4 illustrations. 201pp. 5⅜ x 8½. 23267-0 Pa. $6.95

A SOURCE BOOK IN THEATRICAL HISTORY, A. M. Nagler. Contemporary observers on acting, directing, make-up, costuming, stage props, machinery, scene design, from Ancient Greece to Chekhov. 611pp. 5⅜ x 8½. 20515-0 Pa. $12.95

THE COMPLETE NONSENSE OF EDWARD LEAR, Edward Lear. All nonsense limericks, zany alphabets, Owl and Pussycat, songs, nonsense botany, etc., illustrated by Lear. Total of 320pp. 5⅜ x 8½. (USO) 20167-8 Pa. $7.95

VICTORIAN PARLOUR POETRY: An Annotated Anthology, Michael R. Turner. 117 gems by Longfellow, Tennyson, Browning, many lesser-known poets. "The Village Blacksmith," "Curfew Must Not Ring Tonight," "Only a Baby Small," dozens more, often difficult to find elsewhere. Index of poets, titles, first lines. xxiii + 325pp. 5⅜ x 8¼. 27044-0 Pa. $8.95

DUBLINERS, James Joyce. Fifteen stories offer vivid, tightly focused observations of the lives of Dublin's poorer classes. At least one, "The Dead," is considered a masterpiece. Reprinted complete and unabridged from standard edition. 160pp. 5³⁄₁₆ x 8¼. 26870-5 Pa. $1.00

THE HAUNTED MONASTERY and THE CHINESE MAZE MURDERS, Robert van Gulik. Two full novels by van Gulik, set in 7th-century China, continue adventures of Judge Dee and his companions. An evil Taoist monastery, seemingly supernatural events; overgrown topiary maze hides strange crimes. 27 illustrations. 328pp. 5⅜ x 8½. 23502-5 Pa. $8.95

THE BOOK OF THE SACRED MAGIC OF ABRAMELIN THE MAGE, translated by S. MacGregor Mathers. Medieval manuscript of ceremonial magic. Basic document in Aleister Crowley, Golden Dawn groups. 268pp. 5⅜ x 8¼. 23211-5 Pa. $9.95

NEW RUSSIAN-ENGLISH AND ENGLISH-RUSSIAN DICTIONARY, M. A. O'Brien. This is a remarkably handy Russian dictionary, containing a surprising amount of information, including over 70,000 entries. 366pp. 4½ x 6⅛. 20208-9 Pa. $10.95

HISTORIC HOMES OF THE AMERICAN PRESIDENTS, Second, Revised Edition, Irvin Haas. A traveler's guide to American Presidential homes, most open to the public, depicting and describing homes occupied by every American President from George Washington to George Bush. With visiting hours, admission charges, travel routes. 175 photographs. Index. 160pp. 8¼ x 11. 26751-2 Pa. $11.95

NEW YORK IN THE FORTIES, Andreas Feininger. 162 brilliant photographs by the well-known photographer, formerly with *Life* magazine. Commuters, shoppers, Times Square at night, much else from city at its peak. Captions by John von Hartz. 181pp. 9¼ x 10¾. 23585-8 Pa. $13.95

INDIAN SIGN LANGUAGE, William Tomkins. Over 525 signs developed by Sioux and other tribes. Written instructions and diagrams. Also 290 pictographs. 111pp. 6⅛ x 9¼. 22029-X Pa. $3.95

ANATOMY: A Complete Guide for Artists, Joseph Sheppard. A master of figure drawing shows artists how to render human anatomy convincingly. Over 460 illustrations. 224pp. 8⅜ x 11¼. 27279-6 Pa. $11.95

MEDIEVAL CALLIGRAPHY: Its History and Technique, Marc Drogin. Spirited history, comprehensive instruction manual covers 13 styles (ca. 4th century thru 15th). Excellent photographs; directions for duplicating medieval techniques with modern tools. 224pp. 8⅜ x 11¼. 26142-5 Pa. $12.95

DRIED FLOWERS: How to Prepare Them, Sarah Whitlock and Martha Rankin. Complete instructions on how to use silica gel, meal and borax, perlite aggregate, sand and borax, glycerine and water to create attractive permanent flower arrangements. 12 illustrations. 32pp. 5⅜ x 8½. 21802-3 Pa. $1.00

EASY-TO-MAKE BIRD FEEDERS FOR WOODWORKERS, Scott D. Campbell. Detailed, simple-to-use guide for designing, constructing, caring for and using feeders. Text, illustrations for 12 classic and contemporary designs. 96pp. 5⅜ x 8½. 25847-5 Pa. $3.95

SCOTTISH WONDER TALES FROM MYTH AND LEGEND, Donald A. Mackenzie. 16 lively tales tell of giants rumbling down mountainsides, of a magic wand that turns stone pillars into warriors, of gods and goddesses, evil hags, powerful forces and more. 240pp. 5⅜ x 8½. 29677-6 Pa. $6.95

THE HISTORY OF UNDERCLOTHES, C. Willett Cunnington and Phyllis Cunnington. Fascinating, well-documented survey covering six centuries of English undergarments, enhanced with over 100 illustrations: 12th-century laced-up bodice, footed long drawers (1795), 19th-century bustles, 19th-century corsets for men, Victorian "bust improvers," much more. 272pp. 5⅜ x 8¼. 27124-2 Pa. $9.95

ARTS AND CRAFTS FURNITURE: The Complete Brooks Catalog of 1912, Brooks Manufacturing Co. Photos and detailed descriptions of more than 150 now very collectible furniture designs from the Arts and Crafts movement depict davenports, settees, buffets, desks, tables, chairs, bedsteads, dressers and more, all built of solid, quarter-sawed oak. Invaluable for students and enthusiasts of antiques, Americana and the decorative arts. 80pp. 6½ x 9¼. 27471-3 Pa. $8.95

HOW WE INVENTED THE AIRPLANE: An Illustrated History, Orville Wright. Fascinating firsthand account covers early experiments, construction of planes and motors, first flights, much more. Introduction and commentary by Fred C. Kelly. 76 photographs. 96pp. 8¼ x 11. 25662-6 Pa. $8.95

THE ARTS OF THE SAILOR: Knotting, Splicing and Ropework, Hervey Garrett Smith. Indispensable shipboard reference covers tools, basic knots and useful hitches; handsewing and canvas work, more. Over 100 illustrations. Delightful reading for sea lovers. 256pp. 5⅜ x 8½. 26440-8 Pa. $8.95

FRANK LLOYD WRIGHT'S FALLINGWATER: The House and Its History, Second, Revised Edition, Donald Hoffmann. A total revision–both in text and illustrations–of the standard document on Fallingwater, the boldest, most personal architectural statement of Wright's mature years, updated with valuable new material from the recently opened Frank Lloyd Wright Archives. "Fascinating"–*The New York Times*. 116 illustrations. 128pp. 9¼ x 10¾. 27430-6 Pa. $12.95

CATALOG OF DOVER BOOKS

PHOTOGRAPHIC SKETCHBOOK OF THE CIVIL WAR, Alexander Gardner. 100 photos taken on field during the Civil War. Famous shots of Manassas Harper's Ferry, Lincoln, Richmond, slave pens, etc. 244pp. 10⅝ x 8¼. 22731-6 Pa. $10.95

FIVE ACRES AND INDEPENDENCE, Maurice G. Kains. Great back-to-the-land classic explains basics of self-sufficient farming. The one book to get. 95 illustrations. 397pp. 5⅜ x 8½. 20974-1 Pa. $7.95

SONGS OF EASTERN BIRDS, Dr. Donald J. Borror. Songs and calls of 60 species most common to eastern U.S.: warblers, woodpeckers, flycatchers, thrushes, larks, many more in high-quality recording. Cassette and manual 99912-2 $9.95

A MODERN HERBAL, Margaret Grieve. Much the fullest, most exact, most useful compilation of herbal material. Gigantic alphabetical encyclopedia, from aconite to zedoary, gives botanical information, medical properties, folklore, economic uses, much else. Indispensable to serious reader. 161 illustrations. 888pp. 6½ x 9¼. 2-vol. set. (USO)
Vol. I: 22798-7 Pa. $9.95
Vol. II: 22799-5 Pa. $9.95

HIDDEN TREASURE MAZE BOOK, Dave Phillips. Solve 34 challenging mazes accompanied by heroic tales of adventure. Evil dragons, people-eating plants, blood-thirsty giants, many more dangerous adversaries lurk at every twist and turn. 34 mazes, stories, solutions. 48pp. 8¼ x 11. 24566-7 Pa. $2.95

LETTERS OF W. A. MOZART, Wolfgang A. Mozart. Remarkable letters show bawdy wit, humor, imagination, musical insights, contemporary musical world; includes some letters from Leopold Mozart. 276pp. 5⅜ x 8½. 22859-2 Pa. $7.95

BASIC PRINCIPLES OF CLASSICAL BALLET, Agrippina Vaganova. Great Russian theoretician, teacher explains methods for teaching classical ballet. 118 illustrations. 175pp. 5⅜ x 8½. 22036-2 Pa. $5.95

THE JUMPING FROG, Mark Twain. Revenge edition. The original story of The Celebrated Jumping Frog of Calaveras County, a hapless French translation, and Twain's hilarious "retranslation" from the French. 12 illustrations. 66pp. 5⅜ x 8½. 22686-7 Pa. $3.95

BEST REMEMBERED POEMS, Martin Gardner (ed.). The 126 poems in this superb collection of 19th- and 20th-century British and American verse range from Shelley's "To a Skylark" to the impassioned "Renascence" of Edna St. Vincent Millay and to Edward Lear's whimsical "The Owl and the Pussycat." 224pp. 5⅜ x 8½. 27165-X Pa. $5.95

COMPLETE SONNETS, William Shakespeare. Over 150 exquisite poems deal with love, friendship, the tyranny of time, beauty's evanescence, death and other themes in language of remarkable power, precision and beauty. Glossary of archaic terms. 80pp. $5\frac{3}{16}$ x 8¼. 26686-9 Pa. $1.00

BODIES IN A BOOKSHOP, R. T. Campbell. Challenging mystery of blackmail and murder with ingenious plot and superbly drawn characters. In the best tradition of British suspense fiction. 192pp. 5⅜ x 8½. 24720-1 Pa. $6.95

THE INFLUENCE OF SEA POWER UPON HISTORY, 1660–1783, A. T. Mahan. Influential classic of naval history and tactics still used as text in war colleges. First paperback edition. 4 maps. 24 battle plans. 640pp. 5⅜ x 8½. 25509-3 Pa. $14.95

THE STORY OF THE TITANIC AS TOLD BY ITS SURVIVORS, Jack Winocour (ed.). What it was really like. Panic, despair, shocking inefficiency, and a little heroism. More thrilling than any fictional account. 26 illustrations. 320pp. 5⅜ x 8½. 20610-6 Pa. $8.95

FAIRY AND FOLK TALES OF THE IRISH PEASANTRY, William Butler Yeats (ed.). Treasury of 64 tales from the twilight world of Celtic myth and legend: "The Soul Cages," "The Kildare Pooka," "King O'Toole and his Goose," many more. Introduction and Notes by W. B. Yeats. 352pp. 5⅜ x 8½. 26941-8 Pa. $8.95

BUDDHIST MAHAYANA TEXTS, E. B. Cowell and Others (eds.). Superb, accurate translations of basic documents in Mahayana Buddhism, highly important in history of religions. The Buddha-karita of Asvaghosha, Larger Sukhavativyuha, more. 448pp. 5⅜ x 8½. 25552-2 Pa. $12.95

ONE TWO THREE . . . INFINITY: Facts and Speculations of Science, George Gamow. Great physicist's fascinating, readable overview of contemporary science: number theory, relativity, fourth dimension, entropy, genes, atomic structure, much more. 128 illustrations. Index. 352pp. 5⅜ x 8½. 25664-2 Pa. $8.95

ENGINEERING IN HISTORY, Richard Shelton Kirby, et al. Broad, nontechnical survey of history's major technological advances: birth of Greek science, industrial revolution, electricity and applied science, 20th-century automation, much more. 181 illustrations. ". . . excellent . . ."–*Isis.* Bibliography. vii + 530pp. 5⅜ x 8¼. 26412-2 Pa. $14.95

DALÍ ON MODERN ART: The Cuckolds of Antiquated Modern Art, Salvador Dalí. Influential painter skewers modern art and its practitioners. Outrageous evaluations of Picasso, Cézanne, Turner, more. 15 renderings of paintings discussed. 44 calligraphic decorations by Dalí. 96pp. 5⅜ x 8½. (USO) 29220-7 Pa. $4.95

ANTIQUE PLAYING CARDS: A Pictorial History, Henry René D'Allemagne. Over 900 elaborate, decorative images from rare playing cards (14th–20th centuries): Bacchus, death, dancing dogs, hunting scenes, royal coats of arms, players cheating, much more. 96pp. 9¼ x 12¼. 29265-7 Pa. $12.95

MAKING FURNITURE MASTERPIECES: 30 Projects with Measured Drawings, Franklin H. Gottshall. Step-by-step instructions, illustrations for constructing handsome, useful pieces, among them a Sheraton desk, Chippendale chair, Spanish desk, Queen Anne table and a William and Mary dressing mirror. 224pp. 8⅛ x 11¼. 29338-6 Pa. $13.95

THE FOSSIL BOOK: A Record of Prehistoric Life, Patricia V. Rich et al. Profusely illustrated definitive guide covers everything from single-celled organisms and dinosaurs to birds and mammals and the interplay between climate and man. Over 1,500 illustrations. 760pp. 7½ x 10⅛. 29371-8 Pa. $29.95

Prices subject to change without notice.

Available at your book dealer or write for free catalog to Dept. GI, Dover Publications, Inc., 31 East 2nd St., Mineola, N.Y. 11501. Dover publishes more than 500 books each year on science, elementary and advanced mathematics, biology, music, art, literary history, social sciences and other areas.